dogue de bordeaux

understanding and
caring for your breed

Written by
Myra Lawson

dogue de bordeaux

understanding and
caring for your breed

Written by
Myra Lawson

Pet Book Publishing Company

The Old Hen House St Martin's Farm, Zeals,
Warminster, Wiltshire BA12 6NZ

Printed by Printworks Global Ltd, London & Hong Kong

ISBN: 978-1-910488-44-7

Contents

Introducing the Dogue de Bordeaux

Once seen, never forgotten. The Dogue de Bordeaux's imposing size and forbidding expression may not be to everyone's taste, but he has established an international fan club who think he is the best dog in the world.

Physical characteristics

The Dogue de Bordeaux is a member of the Mastiff family, and all these breeds were developed to be large, powerful and fearless guard dogs. The Dogue is not the largest of the Mastiff breeds, but he is a real powerhouse. His body is strong and muscular and this, combined with his large head, shows that he is a dog to be taken seriously.

Looking front-on, he has a broad, deep chest and a stocky body. His hindquarters are powerful and his tail, which is thick at the root, hangs low.

The Dogue is a true head breed, meaning that this is his outstanding feature. The skull is broad, and is wider at the ears than the eyes.

The muzzle is short but powerful, and the nose is flat; the pendulous lips that overhang powerful jaws are a feature of the breed.

The Dogue's expression is described as "frank" and "forbidding", and this emanates from his wide-set eyes and the wrinkles which appear on either side of a central line, known as the median groove. The wrinkles are most noticeable when he is alert.

Despite his size, the Dogue has an athletic build so he looks as though he is ready to spring into action.

His gait is surprisingly supple for a big dog; he drives from behind and his forelegs have good reach.

The coat is short and fine, and there is one colour for the breed. The Dogue is fawn, although this ranges from dark red mahogany to light fawn.

He may have a black or brown mask, or no mask at all. He may have white marking on his chest and on the paws, but this should not be excessive.

Temperament

In the past, the Dogue de Bordeaux was used for hunting, guarding, fighting, pulling heavy loads and controlling livestock. Today he is honoured as a superb companion dog, but it is important to understand how his temperament has been affected by his working heritage. The Breed Standard, which is a written description of the breed, uses the following terminology to describe his character:

Natural guarding instincts: The Dogue was bred to guard his home and family, and these protective instincts are central to his personality.

Vigilant: The Dogue may appear to be laid back, but don't be fooled. He will always have an eye and an ear tuned to what is going on around him.

Courageous without aggression: This is an important point: the Dogue is fearless which means he will stand his ground, but he will not attack unless severely provoked.

The Dogue de Bordeaux is a natural guard dog.

Good companion: This sounds understated, but what more do you want from a family dog?

Very affectionate: The Dogue is a loyal and loving companion – there are times when you will be literally overpowered by his demonstrations of love.

Snores and slobber!

Not everyone is perfect, and there are a couple of traits that are special to the Dogue de Bordeaux.

The Dogue is a great snorer, which is the result of his foreshortened muzzle and flat nose. This head structure is shared by all brachycephalic breeds, which include the Boxer, Pug and Bulldog. Breathing tends to be more laboured in these breeds, and snoring is therefore inevitable. However, the gentle sounds of a Dogue at rest are all part of his unique charm.

The Dogue also has an undershot jaw, another featured shared by brachycephalic breeds, and this combined with his overhanging lips, creates a lot of slobber. This is no problem to Dogue fans, but you would be advised to keep a towel to hand – especially when visitors are expected!

The ideal home

The Dogue de Bordeaux is a big dog – males weigh in excess of 50kg (110lb) so you need enough space for your Dogue to live in comfort. The garden does need to be extensive as the Dogue is happy to potter or to chill out, although he will remain alert to the comings and goings of the household. He is happy in the town or in the country; indeed, the Dogue adapts well to an urban lifestyle providing he has sufficient exercise coupled with mental stimulation.

The Dogue de Bordeaux adores his family and he will be loving to all members – big or small. He is a sociable type and gets on well with other dogs, although keeping two males is not recommended. The Dogue does have a prey drive, although it tends to vary between individuals. It is therefore advisable to take things very slowly if you have a cat and ensure that interactions are carefully supervised.

The Dogue de Bordeaux is easy to live with – as long as you know what you are doing. This is a powerful dog with a strong guarding instinct; firm and consistent handling is therefore essential. However, with appropriate training and socialisation, the Dogue will mature into a calm and balanced individual, and will be a companion that is second to none.

Tracing back in time

As the name suggests, the Dogue de Bordeaux comes from France where he was used for cattle driving and guarding the vineyards of Bordeaux. However, the origins of the Mastiff family, to which he belongs, go back to ancient times.

The forebears of Mastiffs were known as Mollossers, and dogs of this type were kept by the Assyrians in 700 BC.

Carvings and paintings dating back in time depict them as hunting dogs and guards. Bones of large dogs have also been found in archaeological digs in China, Tibet and India.

Alexander The Great found a new use for these large, powerful dogs; he recruited them to use in his army.

As wars were waged, the army travelled over land and Mollossers found their way to Europe, settling in Italy, Spain and France.

There is additional evidence that a large dog, bearing a striking resemblance to the Dogue de Bordeaux, first existed in Spain.

Known as the Alano, this now extinct breed was brought to Europe by the Alans, a tribe that originated in the Orient.

Separate Identities

As these large Mollossers became established in different countries, they developed more clearly defined roles and established their own identities.

Instead of being known as one type, they emerged as separate breeds, which eventually became the Mastiff, the Bullmastiff, the Tibetan Mastiff, the Neapolitan Mastiff, the Pyrenean Mastiff, the Spanish Mastiff, the Anatolian Shepherd Dog, the Fila Brasileiro and the Dogue de Bordeaux.

Despite his ancient lineage, the history of the Dogue de Bordeaux remains sketchy. It appears that dogs of this type were around at the time of Julius Caesar, and there is strong support for the theory that they arrived in Bordeaux on English trade ships.

The story goes that French locals could not pronounce the word 'dog', and so they became known as Dogue – or Dogue de Bordeaux.

Jack of all trades

Over the ensuing centuries, the French made good use of this versatile dog and he performed a variety of roles with distinction.

He was used for hunting wild boar and was valued by butchers who kept dogs to keep order among steers and for pulling heavy loads of meat from the slaughterhouse to the shops.

In common with many of the Mastiff breeds, the Dogue was also used as a fighting dog, and was pitched against other dogs, bulls and even bears.

However, his size and strength meant that he was always called on as guard and protector of the family. The Dogue de Bordeaux, who was more commonly known as the French Mastiff, was chosen by wealthy families in France to perform this role, and during the French Revolution many dogs lost their lives as they protected their masters to the end.

Developing the breed

The first recorded reference to the Dogue de Bordeaux is in 1863 where the name appears in a French show catalogue – and it was not long before the 'new' breed sparked interest from across the Channel.

In 1886, Dr Frank, the editor of *The Stock keeper*, wrote an article comparing French and English Mastiffs. In his opinion, the dog now known as the Dogue de Bordeaux had retained more of the temperament and courage of the Celtic Mollosser than its English counterpart.

The breed continued to develop in its homeland and was exhibited at the Exposition des Tuileries in Paris in 1892 where a dog called Sultane won the Prix d'Honneur.

This dog was widely recognised as an ideal specimen of the new breed. Dogs were exported to England, and the first class for Dogue de Bordeaux was held in 1896 at the Royal Aquarium in London. A year later, British enthusiasts formed the Dogue de Bordeaux Club, and the breed gained wide admiration.

The three types

The Dogue de Bordeaux was recognised by name but there was still wide variation in type. There is evidence that English-bred Bullmastiffs were sold to France in the late 19th century, and were bred with Dogue de Bordeaux. In addition, there were local variations within France and three distinct types emerged:

Bordeaux type: This included dogs of various coat colours, including brindle, many with extensive white marking.

Some Dogues had a scissor bite, rather than an undershot jaw; there were black masks, red masks, and no masks, and there was variation in head size. However, the Bordeaux type is widely recognised as the Dogue we know today.

Paris type: This type looked more like a Mastiff with a pale, sandy coloured coat. It was smaller than the other types, with a less impressive head.

Toulouse type: Although this type has been described as a 'bad' Great Dane, the true Toulouse type had a powerful, muscular body, very like the Dogue we know today, but the head shape differed with a longer muzzle, a less undershot bite and fewer wrinkles.

Gradually the three types merged as selective breeding established a distinct look, which was cemented with an official Breed Standard.

In the early days, there were regional differences in type and appearance.

Troubled times

Despite its promising start, in the UK, the Dogue de Bordeaux fan base proved fickle, and when a ban on ear cropping was passed, the breed fell from favour. It had lost his gladiatorial look, and subsequently declined in popularity.

The gene pool was small and as interest in the breed dwindled, numbers fell until there were no dogs left in Britain. It was not to return until the end of the 20th century when new dogs were brought in from France. Official recognition was gained in 2001, and from that time onwards, the breed has prospered.

The Dogue is fast becoming the breed of choice for those who want a steadfast and loving companion dog.

The Dogue in the USA

It is thought that the first Dogue de Bordeaux arrived in the USA in the 1890s, but this has not been formally verified. Records start in 1959 when a bitch named Fidelle de Fenelon was imported from France, although there is some thought that she may have been part English Mastiff.

In 1968 Rugby de la Maison, bred by Dr Philip Todd, arrived on the scene, followed by more imports, mostly from Holland. However, the breed was slow to win recognition. The turning point came when a band of enthusiasts established the Dogue de Bordeaux Society of America in 1997, and through their efforts the breed gained official American Kennel Club recognition in 2008. There is now growing interest in the Dogue de Bordeaux which is valued as an impressive show dog and as a loyal and loving companion.

What should a Dogue de Bordeaux look like?

The Dogue de Bordeaux, with his powerful, muscular body and his distinctive head, stands out in any crowd. So what should the perfect Dogue look like?

The aim of breeders is to produce dogs that are sound, healthy, typical examples of their chosen breed in terms of both looks and temperament. To achieve this, they are guided by a Breed Standard, which is a written blueprint describing the perfect specimen.

Of course, there is no such thing as a 'perfect' dog, but breeders aspire to produce dogs that conform as closely as possible to the picture in words presented by the Breed Standard. In the show ring, judges use

the Breed Standard to assess the dogs that come before them, and it is the dog that, in their opinion, comes closest to the ideal, that will win top honours.

This has significance beyond the sport of showing, for it is the dogs that win in the ring which will be used for breeding. The winners of today are therefore responsible for passing on their genes to future generations and preserving the breed in its best form. There are some differences in the wording of the Breed Standard depending on national kennel clubs; the American Kennel Club and the Federation Cynologique Internationale, which is the governing body for 86 countries, have far more descriptive Standards than the brief outline given in the English version.

General appearance

The Dogue de Bordeaux is a strongly built, muscular dog but he remains harmonious in outline, neither leggy, nor too close to the ground. He has a large head – the American Breed Standard asks for a 'massive head" but it should be in proportion with his body. He is a stocky, yet athletic dog, with a forbidding expression which makes him appear imposing.

Temperament

The FCI and the American Standard state that the Dogue de Bordeaux is "gifted for guarding". This is a dog that looks the part, so he can be an effective guard without resorting to aggression. He has the courage to stand his ground, and that is enough to see off most threats. The Dogue is a most lovable creature; he is extremely affectionate and bonds closely with all members of his family.

Head

The Dogue de Bordeaux is a remarkable looking dog and this is mostly because of his head, which is without parallel in the dog world. The Breed Standards give detailed descriptions of the correct proportions, ensuring that this outstanding feature does not become too exaggerated.

The head is wide with a broad forehead. The stop, the step-up between the muzzle and the forehead, is pronounced, the muzzle is short and powerful, and the chin is well defined. The length from the nose to the stop is between a quarter and one-third of the length of the head. The upper lip (flew) is thick and pendulous in profile, showing a rounded lower line. Looking front-on, the edge of the upper lip meets with the lower lip then drops on each side forming a wide, inverted 'V'. The Dogue de Bordeaux is an alert guard, and his forbidding expression is enhanced by the fine, symmetrical wrinkles that form on either side of a central line, known as the median groove.

Eyes

The eyes are oval in shape and set wide apart – the space between is about twice the size of the eye opening. The haw, or third eyelid, should not be visible. The eye colour may vary depending on the mask: hazel to dark brown for dogs with a black mask, lighter eyes are "tolerated but not sought after" for dogs with a brown mask or no mask. The expression is described as "frank".

Ears

The ears are relatively small for the size of head. They are set on high, accentuating the width of the skull. The base is slightly raised, and the ear leathers drop forwards and downwards, but they should not hang limply. The tip of the ear is slightly rounded and should not reach below the level of the eye. When the Dogue is alert, the front edge of the ear lies close to the cheek.

Mouth

The powerful jaws meet in an undershot bite whereby the back of the lower incisors do not come into contact with the upper incisors. The teeth are

Facing page: The typically "frank" gaze of a Dogue de Bordeaux

strong and the lower canines are set wide apart and
are slightly curved.

Neck

The neck is strong and supple, the circumference
almost equals that of the head. It is very broad at
the base, merging smoothly into the shoulders. The
dewlap (loose skin) is well defined, starting at the
throat and flowing in folds down to the forechest.

Forequarters

The Dogue de Bordeaux has a powerful front,
with well-laid, prominent shoulders. The legs are
exceptionally muscled and are as straight as is
compatible with a broad-chested dog.

Body

The chest is broad and powerful and reaches down
below the elbows. The depth of the chest is slightly
more than half of the height of the dog at the withers
(the highest point of the shoulders), and the length
of the body is greater than the height at the withers.
The ribs are well sprung and the back is solid, broad
and muscular.

The topline is level, which should be maintained
when a dog is on the move. The underline is slightly
tucked up.

Despite his muscular build, the Dogue appears harmonious in outline.

Hindquarters

As with the front assembly, the hindquarters are powerful with strong bone. The loin, which is between the last rib and the pelvic bone, is broad, and the croup, which runs from the pelvis to the tail, is short, with a gentle slope leading to the tail. The hind legs are muscular and well angulated.

Feet

The feet are strong with tight toes; the pads are well developed and supple. The hind feet are slightly longer than the front feet.

Despite his weight, the Dogue stands well up on his toes.

Tail

The tail is very thick at the base; the tip should reach to the hock. It is carried low, but when the dog is in action it is raised, although it should never curve over the back.

A kinked tail is considered highly undesirable.

Coat

The coat is short and fine, and is soft to the touch. The skin is thick and loose fitting but wrinkling should not be excessive.

Facing page: A Dogue without a mask will have reddish pigmentation.

Colour

The Dogue de Bordeaux is solid-coloured, and this can be any shade of fawn ranging from mahogany to light fawn. A rich colour is considered an asset. White markings on the chest and paws are permitted but should, ideally, be minimal. The Dogue may or may not have a mask; the colour of the mask will affect pigmentation.

Black mask: This should not extend above the eyes; there may be slight black shading on the ears, skull, neck and topline. The nose is black.

Brown mask: The pigmentation of the nose and eye rims is brown.

No mask: The coat is fawn and the skin and nose are reddish.

Movement

The Dogue de Bordeaux is a big, heavy dog but his movement is free and supple.

He drives from the hindquarters and shows good extension of the forelegs. When the trot quickens, the Dogue tends to drop his head.

Size and weight

The height is measured at the withers – the highest point of the shoulder:

Males: 60-68cm (23.5-26.5in). The American Standard allows for a maximum height of 69cm (27in)

Females: 58-66cm (22.5-26in).

There is a significant difference in weight between the genders:

Males: At least 50kg (110lb)

Females: At least 45kg (99lb).

Summing up

Although the majority of Dogue de Bordeaux are kept as pets and will never be exhibited in the show ring, it is important that breeders strive for perfection and try to produce dogs that adhere as closely as possible to the Breed Standard.

This is most especially true in a breed such as the Dogue de Bordeaux where exaggeration in conformation can lead to serious health issues.

The Dogue de Bordeaux is a very special breed, and it is only by maintaining soundness in mind and body that it can be preserved in its true form, and continue to bring unbounded pleasure to its worldwide fan club for generations to come.

What do you want from your Dogue?

There are over 200 dog breeds to choose from, so how can you be sure that the Dogue de Bordeaux is the right breed for you? Before you decide on a Dogue you need to be 100 per cent confident that this is the breed that is best suited to your lifestyle.

Companion

If you want a loyal, affectionate, steadfast companion, look no further. The Dogue de Bordeaux loves his family and will take enormous delight in being with them.

However, he also feels the need to protect his loved ones, and this instinct needs to be managed. From

this point of view, a Dogue de Bordeaux, particularly a male, is not a good choice for an inexperienced owner.

If you have a family with small children, the Dogue will be an ideal playmate, as long as you establish the ground rules on both sides.

Even as a puppy, the Dogue is big and boisterous and, in no time, he will become a strong and powerful adult.

It is therefore essential that he learns self-control and respects all members of his human family, no matter how small they are.

As far as the children are concerned, they need to understand that a dog needs some quiet times when he is not disturbed, such as when he is eating or sleeping.

He is not a toy to be poked and prodded at will. If these rules are followed and mutual respect is established, a Dogue will become an integral member of the family circle.

Obviously the Dogue's size and strength has a big impact on lifestyle and he would be an unsuitable choice for anyone who is frail or getting on in years.

Sports dog

If you want to become involved in one of the many canine sports now on offer, you may need to think again. The Dogue is a clever dog, but he is not easy to motivate. He can be stubborn and you may find that your relationship deteriorates if you attempt to coerce him into performing tasks that he sees as pointless. However, there are some sports that require a more laid back approach. For more information, see Opportunities for Dogue de Bordeaux.

Show dog

Do you have ambitions to exhibit your Dogue de Bordeaux in the show ring? This is a highly competitive sport so you do need the right dog to begin with. If you plan to show your Dogue you need to track down a show quality puppy, and train him so he will perform in the ring, and accept the detailed 'hands on' examination which is part of the judging process.

It is also important to bear in mind that not every puppy with show potential develops into a top quality specimen, and so you must be prepared to love your Dogue and give him a home for life, even if he doesn't make the grade.

What does your Dogue want from you?

A dog cannot speak for himself, so we need to view the world from a canine perspective and work out what a Dogue de Bordeaux needs in order to live a happy, contented and fulfilling life.

Time and commitment

First of all, a Dogue needs a commitment that you will care for him for the duration of his life, guiding him through his puppyhood, enjoying his adulthood, and being there for him in his later years. If all potential owners were prepared to make this pledge, there would be scarcely any dogs in rescue.

The Dogue de Bordeaux is a superb companion dog, but he does not come readymade. You need to

take charge of his education, guiding him through puppyhood and adolescence, so that he understands his place in the family.

You also need to bear in mind that a Dogue needs to be a fully-fledged member of the family. If he is excluded from family activities or expected to spend lengthy periods on his own, he will not only be thoroughly miserable, he may well invent his own agenda and spend the time barking and whining or being destructive. It is important that all dogs can cope with spending some time on their own so they don't become anxious, but the maximum time a dog should be left is four hours.

If this does not fit in with your lifestyle, you should delay owning a dog until your circumstances change.

Practical matters

The Dogue de Bordeaux is a relatively low maintenance dog when it comes to looking after him. In terms of grooming, his short coat is easy to care for, needing no more than a regular weekly brush. The Dogue is not demanding in terms of exercise, but this does not mean that you should give up on it. The Dogue needs to be kept fit and healthy, and he also needs the mental stimulation that comes with going out and about.

Leadership

The Dogue de Bordeaux is not intrinsically challenging, but he is a dog to be taken seriously. Males, in particular, can be assertive and the instinct to guard needs to be tempered in both sexes.

It is your job to show your Dogue how you want him to behave by rewarding the behaviour that you consider desirable.

You need to be 100 per cent consistent, so he is left in no doubt as to what is deemed acceptable. If he pushes the boundaries or misbehaves, interrupt his undesirable behaviour by ignoring him or refocusing his attention.

As soon as he makes the 'right' decision and changes his behaviour, you can reward him handsomely.

In this way, your Dogue learns good manners without the need for force or confrontation. He is living with you in peace and harmony because he respects you.

Extra considerations

Now you have decided that a Dogue de Bordeaux is the dog of your dreams, you can narrow your choice so you know exactly what you are looking for.

Male or female?

The choice of male or female Dogue comes down to personal preference, but there are some practical considerations. Males are bigger, heavier and more powerful than females – and the female is not exactly a lightweight.

The aim is to teach your Dogue self control so he does not use his physical strength against you, but there are times, particularly during adolescence, when a male takes a lot of handling.

In terms of temperament, both male and female are equally loyal and loving. As already highlighted, the male is more assertive and he requires a more

experienced owner to train and socialise him.

If you choose a female, you will need to cope with her seasons, which will start at around 14 months of age and occur approximately every nine months thereafter. During the three-week period of a season, you will need to keep your bitch away from entire males (males that have not been neutered) to eliminate the risk of an unwanted pregnancy. Some owners also report that females may be a little moody and withdrawn during their seasonal cycle.

Many pet owners opt for neutering, which puts an end to the seasons, and also has many attendant health benefits. The operation, known as spaying, is usually carried out at some point after the first season. The best plan is to seek advice from your vet. An entire male may not cause many problems, although some do have a stronger tendency to mark, which could include inside the house. However, training will usually put a stop to this. An entire male will also be on the lookout for bitches in season, and this may lead to difficulties, depending on your circumstances. Neutering (castrating) a male is a relatively simple operation, and there are associated health benefits. Again, you should seek advice from your vet.

More than one?

Owning Dogue de Bordeaux can be addictive and you may want to expand your canine population. However, think carefully before you go ahead. A Dogue needs training and leadership and you need to have the time to interact with each dog individually as well as doing things together.

Be wary of a breeder who encourages you to buy two puppies from the same litter, as it is unlikely that the welfare of the puppies is their top priority. Pups of the same or similar ages will bond with each other rather than with you – and they will get up to all sorts of mischief. Most responsible breeders have a waiting list of potential purchasers before a litter is even born and have no need to make this type of sale.

If you do decide to take on a second Dogue, wait at least two years – preferably longer – so your first dog is fully trained and settled before embarking on a puppy.

In terms of gender, you should avoid getting two males as they may vie with each other for top dog status. Females are more peaceable but a male/female combination is probably the best option. If you go ahead with this, obviously one or both dogs will need to be neutered.

An older dog

You may decide to miss out on the puppy phase and take on an older dog instead. Such a dog may be harder to track down, but sometimes a breeder may have a youngster that is not suitable for showing, but is perfect for a family pet. In some cases, a breeder may rehome a female when her breeding career is at an end so she will enjoy the benefits of more individual attention. There are advantages to taking on an older dog, as you know exactly what you are getting. But the upheaval of changing homes can be quite upsetting, so you will need to have plenty of patience during the settling in period.

Rehoming a rescued dog

We are fortunate that the number of Dogue de Bordeaux that end up in rescue is relatively small. However, there are dogs that need rehoming through no fault of their own. The reasons are various, ranging from illness or death of the original owner to family breakdown, changing jobs, the arrival of a new baby, or a family may have made the wrong choice and failed to cope with such a large dog. You are highly unlikely to find a Dogue de Bordeaux in an all-breed rescue centre, so contacting a specialist breed club that runs a rescue scheme will be your best option if you decide to go down this route.

Try to find out as much as you can about a dog's history so you know exactly what you are taking on. You need to be aware of age and health status, likes and dislikes, plus any behavioural issues that may be relevant. You need to be realistic about what you are capable of achieving so you can be sure you can give the dog in question a permanent home.

Regardless of the dog's previous history, you will need to give him plenty of time and be patient with him as he settles into his new home. It may take weeks, or even months before he becomes fully integrated in the family, but if all goes well you will have the reward of knowing that you have given a Dogue a second chance.

There is a danger that dogs of a similar age will bond with each other rather than with their human family.

Sourcing a puppy

Your aim is to find a healthy puppy that is typical of the breed, and has been reared with the greatest possible care. Where do you start?

A tried and trusted method of finding a puppy is to attend a dog show where your chosen breed is being exhibited.

This will give you the opportunity to see lots of different Dogue de Bordeaux of all ages. To begin with they may look very much the same, but when you look closely you will detect that there are different 'types' on show.

They are all pure-bred Dogues, but breeders produce dogs with a family likeness, so you can see which type you prefer. When judging has been completed, talk to the exhibitors and find out more about their dogs.

They may not have puppies available, but some will be planning a litter, and you may decide to put your name on a waiting list.

Internet research

The Internet is an excellent resource, but when it comes to finding a puppy, use it with care:

DO go to the website of your national kennel club.

Both the American Kennel Club (AKC) and the Kennel Club (KC) have excellent websites which will give you information about the Dogue de Bordeaux as a breed, and what to look for when choosing a puppy. You will also find contact details for specialist breed clubs (see below).

Both sites have lists of puppies available, and you can look out for breeders of merit (AKC) and assured breeders (KC) which indicates that a code of conduct has been adhered to.

DO find details of specialist breed clubs.

On breed club websites you will find lots of useful information which will help you to care for your Dogue.

There may be contact details of breeders in your area, or you may need to go through the club secretary. Some websites also have a list of breeders that have puppies available. The advantage of going through a breed club is that members will follow a code of ethics, and this will give you some guarantees regarding breeding stock and health checks.

If you are planning to show your Dogue de Bordeaux you will obviously go to a breeder that has had some success in the ring, so you will need to do additional research to discover more about their breeding lines and the type of Dogue they produce.

DO NOT look at puppies for sale.

There are legitimate Dogue de Bordeaux breeders with their own websites, and they may, occasionally,

advertise a litter, although in most cases reputable breeders have waiting lists for their puppies. The danger comes from unscrupulous breeders that produce puppies purely for profit, with no thought for the health of the dogs they breed from and no care given to rearing the litter. Photos of puppies are hard to resist, but never make a decision based purely on an advertisement. You need to find out who the breeder is, and have the opportunity to visit their premises and inspect the litter before making a decision.

Questions, questions, questions

When you find a breeder with puppies available, you will have lots of questions to ask. These should include the following:

- Where have the puppies been reared? Hopefully, they will be in a home environment which gives them the best possible start in life.

- How many are in the litter?

- What is the split of males and females?

- How many have already been spoken for? The breeder will probably be keeping a puppy to show or for breeding, and there may be others on a waiting list.

- Can I see the mother with her puppies?

- What age are the puppies?

- When will they be ready to go to their new homes?

Bear in mind puppies need to be with their mother and siblings until they are eight weeks of age otherwise they miss out on vital learning and communication skills, which will have a detrimental effect on them for the rest of their lives. You should also be prepared to answer a number of searching questions so the breeder can check if you are suitable as a potential owner of one of their precious puppies. You will be asked some or all of the following questions:

- What is your home set up?

- Do you have children/grandchildren?

- What are their ages?

- Do you have a securely fenced garden?

- Is there somebody at home the majority of the time?

- What is your previous experience with dogs?

- Do you already have other dogs at home?

- Do you have plans to show your Dogue?

The breeder is not being intrusive; he needs to understand the type of home you will be able to provide in order to make the right match. Do not be offended by this; the breeder is doing it both for your, and the dog's, benefit.

Steer clear of a breeder who does not ask you questions. He or she may be more interested in making money out of the puppies than ensuring that they go to good homes. They may also have taken other shortcuts which may prove disastrous, and very expensive, in terms of vet bills or plain heartache.

Health issues

In common with all pure-bred dogs, the Dogue de Bordeaux suffers from some hereditary problems so you need to talk to the breeder about the health status of breeding stock and find out if there are any issues of concern.

The Dogue's unusual conformation means that he may suffer pain or discomfort if features of his conformation become exaggerated. In the UK the Dogue de Bordeaux is listed as Category Three or Breed Watch by the Kennel Club, which means that special measures are in place to help breeders eliminate health issues of this type in the breed.

Facing page: The breeder will want to make sure that you can provide a suitable home for a Dogue puppy.

Puppy watching

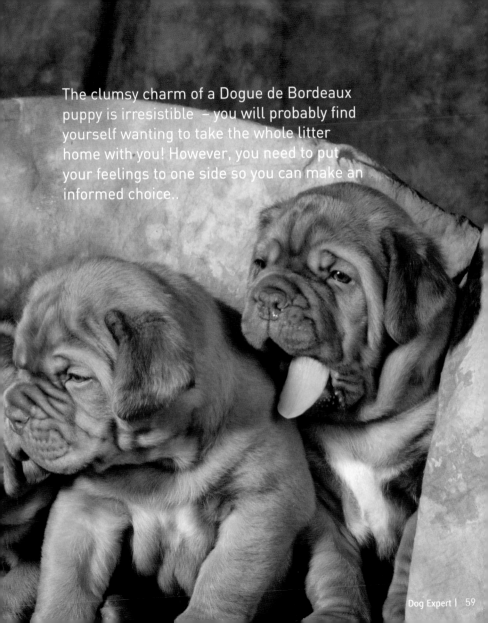

The clumsy charm of a Dogue de Bordeaux puppy is irresistible – you will probably find yourself wanting to take the whole litter home with you! However, you need to put your feelings to one side so you can make an informed choice..

Viewing a litter

It is a good idea to have a mental checklist of what to look out for when you visit a breeder. You want to see:

- A clean, hygienic environment.

- Puppies who are out-going, friendly, and eager to meet you.

- A sweet-natured mother who is ready to show off her pups.

- Puppies that are well covered, but not pot-bellied, which could be an indication of worms.

- Bright eyes, with no sign of soreness or discharge.

- Clean ears that smell fresh.

- No discharge from the ears or the nose.

- Clean rear ends – matting could indicate an upset tummy.

It is important that you see the mother with her puppies as this will give you a good idea of the temperament they are likely to inherit. It is also helpful if you can see other close relatives so you can see the type of Dogue de Bordeaux the breeder produces.

In most cases, you will not be able to see the father

(sire) as most breeders will travel some distance to find a stud dog that is not too close to their own bloodlines and complements their bitch. However, you should be able to see photos of him and be given the chance to examine his pedigree and show record.

Companion puppy

If you are looking for a Dogue de Bordeaux purely as a companion, you should be guided by the breeder who will have spent hours and hours puppy watching, and will know each of the pups as an individual. It is tempting to choose a puppy yourself, but the breeder will take into account your family set up and lifestyle and will help you pick the most suitable puppy.

Show puppy

If you are buying a puppy with the hope of showing him, make sure you make this clear to the breeder. A lot of planning goes into producing a litter, and although all the puppies will have been reared with equal care, there will be one or two that have show potential.

Ideally, recruit a breed expert to inspect the puppies with you so you have the benefit of their objective evaluation. The breeder will also be there to help as they will want to ensure that only the best of their stock is exhibited in the show ring. Wait until the puppies are between seven and eight weeks before making your choice as this gives them time to develop.

It is impossible to say with certainty that a puppy is going to be successful in the show ring; puppies go through many stages when they are growing – and this applies most particularly to the Dogue de Bordeaux which changes more than any of the other Mastiff breeds. However, there are certain guidelines which are worth following:

Watch how the puppies move: you are looking for straight movement at the front and rear.

- A puppy should be relatively short in stature, i.e. low to the ground rather than leggy.

- The head should have the correct proportion: broad at the base of the skull, the correct length of muzzle (one-third of the length of the whole head), and the stop should be at the correct angle to the muzzle. Look for a well-defined chin and the inverted 'V', which is formed by the lips.

- The eyes should be set wide apart, approximately twice the space of eye opening.

- The bite should be undershot, but not too much as this will become excessive in an adult. In some cases a pup will not have the correct bite to begin with, so this feature is notoriously difficult to judge.

- The front legs should be straight with plenty of bone. The chest is low and deep.

- The topline should be straight, and this should be maintained when the puppy moves.

- The rear legs should be straight and parallel, with moderate angulation.

- Check the tail is well formed with no sign of a kink or a knot. It should be set on slightly below the back line to allow for the correct tail carriage.

- All shades of fawn are acceptable, but most exhibitors opt for a darker colour at this stage. White markings should be minimal.

It takes an expert eye to assess show potential.

A Dogue-friendly home

It may seem an age before your Dogue de Bordeaux puppy is ready to leave the breeder and move to his new home. But you can fill the time by getting your home ready, and buying the equipment you will need. These preparations apply to a new puppy but, in reality, they are the means of creating an environment that is safe and secure for your Dogue throughout his life.

In the home

Nothing is safe when a puppy is about, and that is certainly true if you have a Dogue de Bordeaux in the house! Everything is new and exciting for a young puppy, and he will investigate everything with his mouth, which can lead him into all sorts of mischief.

One thing is certain; a free-ranging Dogue puppy

cannot be trusted. Remember, it is not only your prized possessions that are under threat – the damage a puppy can inflict on himself is equally relevant. Trailing electric cables are a major hazard so these will need to be secured out of reach. You will need to make sure all cupboards and storage units cannot be opened or broken into. This applies particularly in the kitchen where you may store cleaning materials, and other substances, which could be toxic to dogs. There are a number of household plants that are poisonous, so these will need to be relocated, along with breakable ornaments.

The Dogue puppy is relatively heavy for his size, and he has a real problem negotiating slippery floor surfaces. If you have a tiled or linoleum floor, you will need to buy some non-slip rugs to allow your puppy a safe passage to and fro. It is all too easy for your pup to be injured at this vulnerable stage.

You will also need to declare upstairs off-limits as going up and down stairs can be hazardous, particularly for a fast growing Dogue puppy. The best way of doing this is to install a baby gate; these can also be useful if you want to limit your Dogue's freedom in any other part of the house. This barrier works well as your dog is separate but does not feel excluded from what is going on.

In the garden

The Dogue de Bordeaux will explore every nook and cranny of your garden, so it needs to be both safe and secure.

Fencing needs to be a minimum of 1.82 m (6ft) in height. You also need to check there are no gaps that he can squeeze through while he is still small. If you have gates leading out of your property, they must have secure fastenings.

If you are a keen gardener, you may want to think about creating an area of garden that is free from plants and shrubs. A Dogue may share your passion for gardening but you are unlikely to appreciate his endeavours. Digging holes and uprooting plants is his idea of helping.

If you allow your Dogue free access to the garden you should be aware that there are a number of plants that are toxic to dogs, such as tulip bulbs, lily of the valley, azaleas, jasmine and daffodil flowers. You can find a comprehensive list on the Internet. You also need to be aware that garden chemicals, such as fertilisers, fungicides and pesticides, are highly toxic so be very careful where you use them.

Swimming pools and ponds should be covered, as most puppies are fearless and, although it is easy for a puppy to take the plunge, it is virtually impossible for him to get out, potentially with lethal consequences.

You will also need to designate a toileting area. This will assist the house training process, and it will also make cleaning up easier.

House rules

Before your puppy comes home, hold a family conference to make the house rules. You need to decide which rooms your puppy will have access to, and establish whether he is to be allowed on the furniture or not. It is important to start as you mean to go on.

You cannot invite a puppy on to the sofa for cuddles only to decide in a few months' time that this is no longer desirable.

The Dogue de Bordeaux is a laid back character but he will push it if he doesn't know where his boundaries lie. In a few months you will be dealing with a large and powerful dog so you need to establish a code of conduct which will avoid future confrontation.

If house rules are applied consistently, your Dogue will understand what is, and what is not, allowed, and he will learn to respect you and co-operate with you.

Facing page: Make sure **you** *decide on the house rules...*

Buying equipment

There are some essential items of equipment you will need for your Dogue de Bordeaux. If you choose wisely, much of it will last for many years to come.

Indoor crate

Rearing a puppy is so much easier if you invest in an indoor crate. It provides a safe haven for your puppy at night, when you have to go out during the day, and at other times when you cannot supervise him. A puppy needs a base where he feels safe and secure, and where he can rest undisturbed. An indoor crate provides the perfect den, and many adults continue to use them throughout their lives.

The crate needs to be large enough for an adult to be able to stand up, turn around, and stretch out in comfort, so the best plan is to buy the biggest crate you can afford. A 122 cm (48 in) crate is recommended.

You will also need to consider where you are going to locate the crate. The kitchen is usually the most suitable place as this is the hub of family life. Try to find a snug corner where the puppy can rest when he wants to, but where he can also see what is going on around him, and still be with the family.

In the car

You will need to work out how you are going to accommodate your Dogue de Bordeaux in the car. An adult Dogue is a substantial animal so it is imperative for everyone's safety that he is safe and secure while travelling. You may opt to buy a crate for the car, which is the most practical option, or you may find that a dog guard will be sufficient.

You will also need to buy a ramp so your Dogue can get in and out of the car without jumping, which will put undue strain on his joints. This is especially important while your Dogue is growing, but it will be useful throughout his life, from puppyhood to old age.

Beds and bedding

The crate will need to be lined with bedding and the best type to buy is synthetic fleece. This is warm and cosy, and as moisture soaks through it, your puppy will not have a wet bed when he is tiny and is still unable to go through the night without relieving himself. This type of bedding is machine washable and easy to dry; buy two pieces, so you have one to use while the other piece is in the wash.

If you have purchased a crate, you may not feel the need to buy an extra bed, although your Dogue may like to have a bed in the family room so he feels part of household activities. There is an amazing array of dog-beds to chose from – duvets, bean bags, cushions, baskets, igloos, mini-four posters – so you can take your pick! However, you do need to bear in mind that a puppy may enjoy chewing his bed, so it is probably worth delaying this purchase until your Dogue has finished teething.

Collar and lead

You may think that it is not worth buying a collar for the first few weeks, but the sooner your pup gets used to it, the better. A nylon lightweight collar is recommended, as most puppies will accept it without making a fuss. Be careful when you are fitting the collar that it is not too tight, but equally not too loose, as slipping the collar can become a favourite game. As your puppy gets bigger and stronger, you may find that a half-check collar will give you better control. A harness is another option; a correct fit is important to ensure that it doesn't rub and your Dogue is comfortable.

A matching webbing lead will be fine to begin with but as your Dogue grows you will need something more substantial. Most Dogue owners opt for a strong leather lead, which does not chafe the hands. Again, there are plenty to choose from; the most important consideration is that the lead has a secure trigger fastening.

A permanent form of ID is now a legal requirement.

An extending lead can be a useful purchase as you can give your Dogue limited freedom when it is not safe or permitted to allow him off lead. However, you should never use it when walking alongside roads as an unexpected pull from your Dogue resulting in the lead extending further than you want, could have disastrous consequences.

ID

Your Dogue de Bordeaux needs to wear some form of ID when he is out in public places. This can be in the form of a disc, engraved with your contact details, attached to the collar. When he is full-grown, you can buy a collar embroidered with your contact details, which eliminates the danger of the disc becoming detached from the collar. It is now mandatory for your dog to have a permanent form of ID, which usually comes in the form of a microchip. Increasingly breeders are getting puppies microchipped before they go to their new homes.

A microchip is the size of a grain of rice. It is injected under the skin, usually between the shoulder blades, with a special needle. It has tiny barbs on it, which dig into the tissue around where it lies, so it does not migrate from that spot.

Each chip has its own unique identification number which can only be read by a special scanner. That ID number is then registered on a national database with your name and details, so that if ever your dog is lost, he can be taken to any vet or rescue centre where he is scanned and then you are contacted.

If your puppy has not been microchipped, you can ask your vet to do it, maybe when he goes for his vaccinations.

Bowls

Your Dogue will need two bowls; one for food, and one for fresh drinking water, which should always be readily available. A stainless steel bowl is a good choice for food as it is tough and hygienic.

Plastic bowls will almost certainly be chewed, and there is a danger that bacteria can collect in the small cracks that may appear. You can opt for a second stainless steel bowl for drinking water, or you may prefer a heavier ceramic bowl which will not be knocked over so easily.

Toys need to be tough

Food

The breeder will let you know what your puppy is eating and should provide a full diet sheet to guide you through the first six months of your puppy's feeding regime – how much he is eating per meal, how many meals per day, when to increase the amounts given per meal and when to reduce the meals per day.

The breeder may provide you with some food when you go and collect your puppy, but it is worth making enquiries in advance about the availability of the brand that is recommended.

Grooming gear

The Dogue is a low maintenance breed in terms of coat care but there are a few essentials you will need:

- Soft brush: To use while your puppy is becoming accustomed to grooming.

- Stiff bristle brush: For the adult coat.

- Chamois leather: To bring out the shine in the coat.

- Hand towels: To wipe away excess slobber!

- Nail-clippers: The guillotine type are easy to use.

- Toothbrush and toothpaste: Choose between a long-handled toothbrush or a finger brush – whichever you find easiest to use. There are flavoured canine toothpastes on the market which are acceptable to your dog.

Toys

A Dogue puppy will be playful, and the more you play with him, the more he is likely to enjoy the interaction. But before you get carried away with buying a vast range of toys to keep your puppy entertained, think about possible hazards.

A puppy can easily chew bits from soft or plastic toys, and if this material is ingested it can cause serious problems in the form of a blockage.

The safest toys to choose are made of hard rubber; a rubber kong which can be stuffed with food is ideal.

You can also buy rope tug toys, but be careful how you play with your dog, particularly while he is teething.

Finding a vet

Before your puppy arrives home, you should register with a vet. Visit several vets in your local area, or speak to other pet owners that you might know, to see who they recommend.

It is so important to find a good vet – almost as much as finding a good doctor for yourself. You need to find someone with whom you can build up a good rapport and have complete faith in. Word of mouth is really the best recommendation.

When you contact a veterinary practice, find out the following:

- Does the surgery run an appointment system?

- What are the arrangements for emergency, out of hours cover?

- Do any of the vets in the practice have experience treating Dogue de Bordeaux?

- What facilities are available at the practice?

If you are satisfied with what you find, and the staff appear to be helpful and friendly, book an appointment so your puppy can have a health check a couple of days after you collect him.

Facing page: You are responsible for your Dogue's health and wellbeing from the moment he arrives in his new home.

Settling in

When you first arrive home with your puppy, be careful not to overwhelm him. You and your family are hugely excited, but the puppy is in a completely strange environment with new sounds, smells and sights, which is a daunting experience, even for the boldest of pups.

Some puppies are very confident, wanting to play straightaway and quickly making friends; others need a little longer. Keep a close check on your puppy's body language and reactions so you can proceed at a pace he is comfortable with.

First, let him explore the garden. He will probably need to relieve himself after the journey home, so take him to the allocated toileting area and, when he performs, give him plenty of praise.

When you take your puppy indoors, let him investigate again. Show him his crate, and encourage him to go in by throwing in a treat. Let

him have a sniff, and allow him to go in and out as he wants to. Later on, when he is tired, you can put him in the crate while you stay in the room. In this way he will learn to settle and will not think he is being abandoned.

It is a good idea to feed your puppy in his crate, at least to begin with, as this helps to build up a positive association. It will not be long before your Dogue sees his crate as his own special den and will go there as a matter of choice. Some owners place a blanket over the crate, covering the back and sides, so that it is even more cosy and den-like.

Meeting the family

Resist the temptation of inviting friends and neighbours to come and meet the new arrival; your puppy needs to focus on getting to know his new family for the first few days. Try not to swamp your Dogue with too much attention; give him a chance to explore and find his feet. There will be plenty of time for cuddles later on!

If you have children in the family, you need to keep everything as calm as possible. Your puppy may not have met children before, and even if he has, he will still find them strange and unpredictable. A puppy can become alarmed by too much noise, or he may go to the opposite extreme and become over-excited, which can lead to mouthing and nipping. The best plan is to get the children to sit on the floor and give them all a treat. Each child can then call the puppy, stroke him, and offer a treat. In this way the puppy is making the decisions rather than being forced into interactions he may find stressful. If he tries to nip or mouth, make sure there is a toy at the ready, so his attention can be diverted to something he is allowed to bite. If you do this consistently, he will learn to inhibit his desire to mouth when he is interacting with people.

Right from the start, impose a rule that the children are not allowed to pick up or carry the puppy. They can cuddle him when they are sitting on the floor. This may sound a little severe, but a wriggly puppy can be dropped in an instant, sometimes with disastrous consequences. If possible, try to make sure your Dogue is only given attention when he has all four feet on the ground.

That sweet little puppy will soon become a powerful adult and you need to establish the fact that jumping up is non-productive. Involve all family members with the day-to-day care of your puppy; this will enable the bond to develop with the whole family as opposed to just one person. Encourage the children to train and reward the puppy, teaching him to follow their commands without question.

The animal family

Care must be taken when introducing a puppy to a resident dog to ensure that relations get off on the right footing. The Dogue de Bordeaux does not go looking for trouble, but it is always better to take things slowly.

Your adult dog may be allowed to meet the puppy at the breeder's, which is ideal as the older dog will not feel threatened if he is away from home.

But if this is not possible, allow your dog to smell the puppy's bedding (the bedding supplied by the breeder is fine) before they actually meet so he familiarises himself with the puppy's scent.

The garden is the best place for introducing the puppy, as the adult will regard it as neutral territory. He will probably take a great interest in the puppy and sniff him all over.

Most puppies are naturally submissive in this situation, and your pup may lick the other dog's mouth or roll over on to his back. Try not to interfere as this is the natural way that dogs get to know each other.

You will only need to intervene if the older dog is too boisterous, and alarms the puppy. In this case, it is a good idea to put the adult on his lead so you have some measure of control. It rarely takes long for an adult to accept a puppy, as he does not constitute a threat. This will be underlined if you make a big fuss of the older dog so that he has no reason to feel jealous. But no matter how well the two dogs are getting on, do not leave them alone unless one is crated.

The Dogue de Bordeaux is a tolerant animal and will enjoy canine company – big or small.

Feline friends

The Dogue de Bordeaux was used as a hunting dog, and while some individuals have a strong prey drive, others show very little interest in chasing. However, it is better to be safe than sorry, so proceed with caution until you have established mutual tolerance between the two.

It may be easier if the cat is confined in a carrier for the first couple of meetings so your puppy has a chance to make his acquaintance in a controlled situation.

Keep calling your puppy to you and rewarding him so that he does not focus too intently on the cat. You can then graduate to holding your puppy while the cat is free, again rewarding him with a treat every time he responds to you and looks away from the cat. When you allow your puppy to go free, make sure the cat has an easy escape route, just in case he tries to chase.

This is an on-going process but, all the time your Dogue is learning that he is rewarded for ignoring the cat. In time, the novelty will wear off and the pair will mostly ignore each other. In some cases, a Dogue and the family cat will become the best of friends and end up sharing a bed!

Prey drive does vary between individuals so it is best to err on the side of caution.

Feeding

The breeder will generally provide enough food for the first few days so the puppy does not have to cope with a change in diet – and possible digestive upset – along with all the stress of moving home.

Some puppies eat up their food from the first meal onwards, others are more concerned by their new surroundings and are too distracted to eat. The Dogue de Bordeaux likes his food but he is not obsessed by it, so he may be reluctant to eat in the first few days.

If this is the case, give him 10 minutes to eat what he wants and then remove the leftovers and start afresh at the next meal. Obviously if you have any concerns about your puppy in the first few days, seek advice from your vet.

It is important to give your dog space where he can eat in peace, and if you have children, you need to establish a rule that no one is to go near the dog when he is feeding.

However, the Dogue does have a guarding streak so you must ensure that he does not become possessive about his food. The best strategy is to give him half his ration, and then drop food around his bowl. This will stop him guarding his bowl and, at the same time, he will see your presence in a positive light. You can also call him away from the bowl and reward him with food – maybe something extra special – which he can take from your hand. Start doing this as soon as your puppy arrives in his new home, and continue working on it throughout his life.

Establish a bedtime routine so your puppy learns to settle.

The first night

Your puppy will have spent the first weeks of his life with either his mother or curled up with his siblings. He is then taken from everything he knows as familiar, lavished with attention by his new family, and then comes bed time when he is left all alone. It is little wonder that he feels abandoned. The best plan is to establish a nighttime routine, and

then stick to it so that your puppy knows what is expected of him. Take your puppy out into the garden to relieve himself, and then settle him in his crate.

Some people leave a low light on for the puppy at night for the first week, others have tried a radio as company or a ticking clock. A covered hot-water bottle, filled with warm water, can also be a comfort.

Like people, puppies are all individuals and what works for one, does not necessarily work for another, so it is a matter of trial and error.

Be very positive when you leave your puppy on his own; do not linger, or keep returning; this will make the situation more difficult. It is inevitable that he will protest to begin with, but if you stick to your routine, he will accept that he gets left at night but you always return in the morning.

Rescued dogs

Settling an older, rescued dog in the home is very similar to a puppy in as much as you will need to make the same preparations regarding his homecoming. As with a puppy, an older dog will need you to be consistent, so start as you mean to go on.

There is often an initial honeymoon period when you bring a rescued dog home, where he will be on his best behaviour for the first few weeks.

It is after these first couple of weeks that the true nature of the dog will show, so be prepared for subtle changes in his behaviour. It may be advisable to register with a reputable training club, so you can seek advice on any training or behavioural issues at an early stage.

Above all, remember that a rescued dog ceases to be a rescued dog the moment he enters his forever home and should be treated normally like any other family pet.

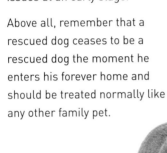

An older dog needs time to adjust to his new home.

House training

This is an aspect of training that first-time owners dread, but if you start as you mean to go on, it will not be long before your Dogue de Bordeaux understands what is required.

The key to successful house training is vigilance and consistency. If you establish a routine, and you stick to it, your puppy will understand what is required.

Equally, you must be there to supervise him at all times, except when he is safely tucked up in his crate. It is when a puppy is left to wander from room to room that accidents are most likely to happen.

As discussed earlier, you will have allocated a toileting area in your garden when preparing for your puppy's homecoming. You need to take your puppy to this area every time he needs to relieve himself. In this way he builds up an association and knows why you have brought him out to the garden.

Establish a routine and make sure you take your puppy out at the following times:

- First thing in the morning

- After mealtimes

- On waking from a sleep

- Following a play session

- Last thing at night.

A puppy should be taken out to relieve himself every two hours as an absolute minimum. If you can manage an hourly trip out, so much the better.

The more often your puppy gets it right, the quicker he will learn to be clean in the house. It helps if you use a verbal cue, such as 'Busy', when your pup is performing and, in time, this will trigger the desired response.

Do not be tempted to put your puppy out on the doorstep in the hope that he will toilet on his own. Most pups simply sit there, waiting to get back inside the house!

No matter how bad the weather is, accompany your puppy and give him lots of praise when he performs correctly. Do not rush back inside as soon as he has finished; your puppy might start to delay in the hope of prolonging his time outside with you.

Praise him, have a quick game, and then you can both return indoors.

When accidents happen

No matter how vigilant you are, there are bound to be accidents. If you witness the accident, take your puppy outside immediately, and give him lots of praise if he finishes his business out there.

If you are not there when he has an accident, do not scold him when you discover what has happened. He will not remember what he has done and will not understand why you are cross with him. Simply clean it up and resolve to be more vigilant next time.

Make sure you use a deodoriser, available in pet stores, when you clean up otherwise your pup will be drawn to the smell and may be tempted to use the same spot again.

Choosing
a diet

There are so many different types of dog food on sale, all claiming to be the best, so how do you know what is likely to suit your Dogue de Bordeaux?

When choosing a diet, there are basically three categories to choose from:

Complete

This is probably the most popular diet as it is easy to feed and is specially formulated with all the nutrients your dog needs. This means that you should not add any supplements or you may upset the nutritional balance.

Most complete diets come in different life stages: puppy, adult maintenance and senior, so this means that your Dogue is getting what he needs when he is growing, during adulthood, and as he becomes older.

You can even get prescription diets for dogs with

particular health issues. Check protein levels provided in the diet; it is important that your Dogue has the correct level depending on his age and lifestyle.

Puppies and juniors need 25-35 per cent of protein in the diet for growth and development; 18-20 per cent protein is adequate for adult maintenance; working dogs and lactating bitches need a higher level, around 25-28 per cent, and veterans needs a much lower level, decreasing from the basic adult maintenance diet.

There are many different brands to choose from so it is advisable to seek advice from your puppy's breeder who will have lengthy experience of feeding Dogue de Bordeaux.

Canned/pouches

This type of food is usually fed with hard biscuit, and most Dogue de Bordeaux find it very appetising.

However, the ingredients and the nutritional value do vary significantly between the different brands so you will need to check the label.

This type of food often has a high moisture content, so make sure your Dogue is getting all the nutrition he requires.

Homemade

There are some owners who like to prepare meals especially for their dogs – and it is probably much appreciated. The danger is that although the food is tasty, and your Dogue may appreciate the variety, you cannot be sure that it has the correct nutritional balance.

If this is a route you want to go down, you will need to find out the exact ratio of fats, carbohydrates, proteins, minerals and vitamins that are needed, which is quite an undertaking.

The Barf (Biologically Appropriate Raw Food) diet is another, more natural approach to feeding. Dogs are fed a diet mimicking what they would have eaten in the wild, consisting of raw meat, bone, muscle, fat, and vegetable matter.

Dogue de Bordeaux do very well on this diet so it is certainly worthy of consideration. There are now a number of companies that specialise in producing the Barf diet in frozen form, which will make your job a lot easier.

Feeding regime

When your puppy arrives in his new home he will need four meals, evenly spaced throughout the day. You may decide to keep to the diet recommended by your puppy's breeder, and if your pup is thriving there is no need to change.

However, if your puppy is not doing well on the food, or you have problems with supply, you will need to make a change.

When switching diets, it is very important to do it on a gradual basis, changing over from one food to the next, a little at a time, and spreading the transition over a week to 10 days. This will avoid the risk of digestive upset.

From about 12 weeks, you can go down to three meals a day, and by six months, you can feed twice daily – a regime which should suit your Dogue for the rest of his life. There are those that advocate feeding one meal a day, but this may increase the likelihood of gastric torsion, also known as bloat.

This is a life threatening condition where the gut twists and fills with air.

Emergency surgery is the only hope of survival. It is thought that overloading the stomach could be a potential risk, and exercising immediately before and after feeding should be avoided.

To err on the side of caution, leave a minimum of one hour either side of exercise.

Food scatter

Mealtimes are the highlight of your Dogue's day –
but it is all over in a matter of minutes. However,
you can prolong his enjoyment – and provide mental
stimulation – by allowing him to forage. Instead
of giving your Dogue his food in a bowl, scatter it
over a small area in the garden and give him the
opportunity to find it. He will relish the opportunity
to use his nose – and the result will be highly
rewarding.

A food scatter is a useful device to use on days
when exercise may have been limited, or simply as
a means of giving your intelligent dog an occupation
he will enjoy.

*Do not exercise your
Dogue immediately
before, or after, feeding.*

Faddy feeders

The Dogue de Bordeaux generally has a good appetite; if this changes it could be a sign that he is unwell and you may need to seek advice. However, there will always be the Dogue who thinks it is worth pushing his luck in the hope that you may provide superior food.

The moment your Dogue looks at you with a furrowed brow, you will be stirred to greater efforts, determined to find a food he may like. At first you may add some gravy, then you may try some chicken... A clever Dogue will quickly realise that if he holds out, tastier treats will follow.

This is a bad game to play as not only will you run out of tempting delicacies, you will also be losing your Dogue's respect.

If your Dogue is turning up his nose at mealtimes, give him 10 minutes to eat what he wants, and then take up his bowl.

Do not feed him treats in between meals, and give him fresh food at his next mealtime. If you continue this regime for a couple of days, your Dogue will realise that there is no percentage in holding out for better food as it never materialises.

In most cases, this is just a 'trying it on' phase, and

It is your job to provide a balanced diet, depending on your Dogue's individual needs.

if you cope with common sense, you will soon return to the status quo and your Dogue will be content with his normal rations.

If, however, your dog refuses all food for more than 24 hours you need to observe his behaviour to see if there are any signs of ill health, which may involve the need for a veterinary check up.

Bones and chews

Puppies love to chew, and many adults also enjoy gnawing on a bone. A raw marrow bone is ideal, but make sure it is always given under supervision.

White, sterilised bones do not make so much mess as a raw marrow bone, and they have the same end result of helping to keep your dog's teeth clean.

Antler chews are a popular choice, and they do seem to last a long time – even when the powerful jaws of a Dogue are at work!

Rawhide chews are best avoided; it is all too easy for a Dogue to bite off a chunk and swallow it, with the danger of it then causing a blockage.

Ideal weight

In order to help to keep your Dogue de Bordeaux in good health it is necessary to monitor his weight. If your dog gets sufficient exercise and is fed a diet that matches his energy output, he should not put on weight. But it is something you should monitor closely.

A dog that is carrying too much weight is vulnerable to many health issues; he has a reduced quality of life as he cannot exercise properly, and he will almost certainly have a reduced life expectancy.

When judging your Dogue's condition, look at him from above, and make sure you can see a definite waist. You should be able to feel his ribs, but not see them.

If you are concerned about your Dogue's weight, get into the habit of visiting your veterinary surgery on a monthly basis so that you can weigh him. You can keep a record of his weight so you can make adjustments if necessary.

If you are worried that your Dogue is putting on too much weight, or equally if you think he is underweight, consult your vet who will help you to plan a suitable diet.

Caring for your Dogue De Bordeaux

The Dogue de Bordeaux is classed as a low maintenance breed but, like all animals, he has his own special needs which you need to take on board.

Coat care

The shorthaired Dogue de Bordeaux needs minimal grooming – and a puppy requires even less – but do not make the mistake of ignoring this aspect of his care.

A grooming session gives you the opportunity to check your dog and to discover any minor problems, such as sore places, or any abnormalities, such as lumps and bumps, which may need to be investigated.

Remember, if you spot a problem early on, you increase the chance of an early diagnosis and a successful outcome.

Bear in mind, your Dogue de Bordeaux puppy is soon going to be very large indeed so he needs to become accustomed to handling before he attempts to use his strength against you.

Initially, he will wriggle and attempt to mouth you, but just ignore his protests. Hold him steady for a few moments, and reward him when he is still. A puppy needs to learn that it is OK to be touched all over; if you fail to do this, he may try to warn you off by growling, which could develop into more problematic behaviour.

Start by handling your puppy all over, stroking him from his head to his tail. Lift up each paw in turn, and reward him with a treat when he co-operates.

Then roll him over on to his back and tickle his tummy; this is a very vulnerable position for a dog to adopt, so do not force the issue. Be firm but gentle, and give your Dogue lots of praise when he does as you ask.

When your Dogue is happy to be handled in this way, you can introduce a soft brush and spend a few minutes working on his coat, and then reward him. He will gradually learn to accept the attention, and will relax while you groom him.

When the adult coat comes through it will be short and fine. A bristle brush is ideal for keeping the coat in good order as it gets rid of dirt and debris; brushing also has a beneficial massaging effect.

If you are exhibiting your Dogue de Bordeaux in the show ring, or you want him to look his very best, give him a rub down with a chamois leather – this will really bring out the sheen in his coat.

Bathing

A Dogue de Bordeaux should not be bathed too frequently as it has an adverse effect on the skin's natural oils. Not only does this result in a dull coat, it can also cause a dry, itchy skin. However, there are times when your Dogue decides to roll in something particularly revolting, and you have no option but to bath him. Make sure you use a mild moisturising shampoo specially formulated for dogs, and you can also use a conditioner which will improve the quality and appearance of the coat.

It is essential to plan the first bath while your Dogue is still small enough to handle easily. He will then become accustomed to the procedure and bath times will not become a battlefield.

Routine care

In addition to grooming, you will need to carry out some routine care.

Eyes

Check the eyes for signs of soreness or discharge. You can use a piece of cotton wool (cotton) – a separate piece for each eye – and wipe away any debris.

Ears

The ears should be clean and free from odour. You can buy specially manufactured ear wipes, or you can use a piece of cotton wool (cotton) to clean them if necessary. Do not probe into the ear canal or you risk doing more harm than good.

The Dogue's coat is low maintenance but regular grooming is beneficial.

Facial folds

The wrinkles or facial folds should not be exaggerated but, even so, they should be routinely cleaned and then dried, so they do not become a source of infection.

Teeth

Dental disease is becoming more prevalent among dogs so teeth cleaning should be seen as an essential part of your care regime.

The build up of tartar on the teeth can result in tooth decay, gum infection and bad breath, and if it is allowed to accumulate, you may have no option but to get the teeth cleaned under anaesthetic.

When your Dogue is still a puppy, accustom him to teeth cleaning so it becomes a matter of routine.

Dog toothpaste comes in a variety of meaty flavours, which your Dogue will like, so you can start by putting some toothpaste on your finger and gently rubbing his teeth. You can then progress to using a finger brush or a toothbrush, whichever you find most convenient.

Remember to reward your Dogue when he co-operates and then he will positively look forward to his teeth-cleaning sessions.

Nails

Nail trimming is a task dreaded by many owners, and many dogs, but if you start early on, your Dogue will get used to the task you have to perform and will not fight against it. If your dog has light-coloured nails, which will often be the case if he has white tips to his toes, you will be able to see the quick (the vein that runs through the nail).

This must be avoided at all costs. If you cut the quick it will bleed profusely and cause considerable discomfort. If your dog has dark nails, you will be unable to see the quick, which makes the task more difficult. The best policy is to trim little and often so the nails don't grow too long, and you do not risk cutting too much and catching the quick. If you are worried about trimming your Dogue's nails, go to your vet so you can see it done properly. If you are still concerned, you can always use the services of a professional groomer.

Exercise

In common with the other Mastiff breeds, the Dogue de Bordeaux does not need extensive exercise. These dogs are strong, powerful and heavy, and although the Dogue has a relatively athletic build, he prefers to take life at a leisurely pace.

While your Dogue is growing, he will be vulnerable to injury caused by putting excessive strain on the joints.

For this reason, exercise should be limited; he also needs to avoid going up and down stairs or jumping in and out of the car. Initially, he will get as much exercise as he needs playing in the garden, and this can be stepped up gradually when he has completed his vaccination course.

Remember, a 10-minute walk on the lead is exhausting for a youngster, particularly if it is on a hard surface. You need to plan your outings so your puppy has a mixture of lead walking and free running – but always err on the side of caution, ending the expedition before your Dogue begins to tire.

When your Dogue is fully grown, he will enjoy a regime of daily exercise which will keep him fit and healthy. This will have the opportunity to see new sights, and when he is off-lead he can investigate the world of scent, which holds great fascination for all dogs.

An adult Dogue is not especially motivated by toys, but some will retrieve or play hide-and-seek, looking for treats or a toy, which provides additional mental stimulation.

Facing page: Your Dogue will enjoy a variety of exercise...

The older Dogue

Unfortunately, the Dogue de Bordeaux is not the most long-lived of breeds. Some reach double figures, but there is no guarantee. Regardless of his health status, a Dogue is likely to show signs of ageing from seven onwards.

As your Dogue grows older, he may sleep more and he may be reluctant to go for longer walks. He may show signs of stiffness when he gets up from his bed, but these generally ease when he starts moving. Some older Dogue de Bordeaux may have impaired vision, and some may become a little deaf, but as long as their senses do not deteriorate dramatically, this is something older dogs learn to live with.

If you treat your older dog with kindness and consideration, he will enjoy his later years and suffer the minimum of discomfort.

It is advisable to switch him over to a senior diet, which is more suited to his needs, and you may need to adjust the quantity, as he will not be burning up the calories as he did when he was younger and more energetic.

The older Dogue will often prefer a softer diet, and you will need to keep a close check on his teeth as these may cause problems. Make sure his sleeping quarters are warm and free from draughts, and if he gets wet, make sure you dry him thoroughly.

Most important of all, be guided by your Dogue. He will have good days when he feels up to going for a walk, and other days when he would prefer to potter in the garden.

If you have a younger dog at home, this may well stimulate him to take more of an interest in what is going on, but make sure he is not pestered as he needs to rest undisturbed when he is tired.

Enjoy the special times you will spend with your Dogue as he grows older.

Letting go

Inevitably there comes a time when your Dogue is not enjoying a good quality of life, and you need to make the painful decision to let him go. We would all wish that our dogs died, painlessly, in their sleep but, unfortunately, this is rarely the case.

However, we can allow our dogs to die with dignity, and to suffer as a little as possible, and this should be our way of saying thank you for the wonderful companionship they have given us.

When you feel the time is drawing close, talk to your vet who will be able to make an objective assessment of your Dogue's condition and will help you to make the right decision.

This is the hardest thing you will ever have to do as a dog owner, and it is only natural to grieve for your beloved Dogue.

But eventually you will be able to look back on the happy memories of times spent together, and this will bring much comfort. You may, in time, feel that your life is not complete without a Dogue de Bordeaux, and you will feel ready to welcome a new puppy into your home.

Facing page: Your Dogue has the right to enjoy a reasonable quality of life – right to the end.

|Social skills

To live in the modern world, without fears and anxieties, your Dogue de Bordeaux needs to receive an education in social skills so that he learns to cope calmly and confidently in a wide variety of situations. The Dogue de Bordeaux has natural guarding instincts, and this may lead to problematic behaviour without the appropriate socialisation and training.

Early learning

The breeder will have begun a programme of socialisation by getting the puppies used to all the sights and sounds of a busy household. You need to continue this when your pup arrives in his new home, making sure he is not worried by household equipment, such as the vacuum cleaner or the washing machine, and that he gets used to unexpected noises from the radio and television.

To begin with, your puppy needs to get used to all the

members of his new family, but then you should give him the opportunity to meet friends and other people who visit your home. If you do not have children, make sure your puppy has the chance to meet and play with other people's children, making sure interactions are always supervised, so he learns that people come in small sizes too. The Dogue de Bordeaux will become deeply attached to his home and family, and this is one of the great assets of the breed. However, a desire to protect the family, stemming from his origins as a guard dog, can lead to problems if it is unchecked.

Your Dogue needs to look to you for guidance so that he does not feel the need to make his own decisions. So, if you welcome a visitor to your home, he will know it is OK to make friends. The aim is for your Dogue to respect you in such a way that he never feels he has to take the lead. It is important to bear in mind that the Dogue is not an aggressive dog; in fact, he will only show aggressive behaviour if he is very severely provoked.

However you are dealing with a strong-willed dog and males, particularly during adolescence, are inclined to push the boundaries. You need to be entirely consistent in your handling so your Dogue accepts your decisions without question. One of your most important jobs is to teach your Dogue good manners so that he remains calm and does not feel that visitors pose a threat. You can do this by adopting the following training programme: If your Dogue has a tendency to jump up and 'mug' visitors, keep him on a lead and make sure he is sitting before he is given any attention. As your Dogue learns to control his behaviour you can ask the visitor to give him a treat – but only when he is sitting and behaving calmly.

If your Dogue is showing guarding behaviour when visitors come to the house, adopt the same strategy outlined above, firstly rewarding your Dogue for being calm and quiet and then allowing the visitor to give him a treat. In this way, you are making the decisions and your Dogue will accept your leadership rather than taking the law into his own hands.

The outside world

When your puppy has completed his vaccinations, he is ready to venture into the outside world. Dogue de Bordeaux are generally pretty confident but there is a lot for a youngster to take on board, so do not swamp him with too many new experiences when you first set out. Obviously you need to work at lead-training before you go on your first expedition. There will be plenty of distractions, so you do not want the additional problem of coping with a dog that is pulling or lagging on the lead.

Hopefully, you can set off with your Dogue walking by your side on a loose lead. He may need more encouragement when you venture further afield, so arm yourself with some extra special treats, which will give him a good reason to focus on you when required!

Start socialising your puppy in a quiet area with light traffic, and only progress to a busier place when he is ready. There is so much to see and hear – people (maybe carrying bags or umbrellas), pushchairs, bicycles, cars, lorries, machinery – so give your puppy a chance to take it all in.

If he does appear worried, do not fall into the trap of sympathising with him or over-doing the reassurance. This will only teach your pup that he had a good reason to be worried and, with luck, you will rescue him if he feels scared. Equally, do not attempt to force him; the Dogue de Bordeaux has a stubborn side and he will dig in his heels if he feels coerced. Instead, give him a little space so he does not have to confront whatever he is frightened of, and distract him with a few treats. Then coax him to walk past, using an encouraging tone of voice, never forcing him by yanking on the lead. Reward him for

Facing page: You want your Dogue de Bordeaux to take all new situations in his stride.

any forward movement, and your puppy will soon learn that he can trust you, and there is nothing to fear.

Your pup also needs to continue his education in canine manners, started by his mother and by his littermates, as it is essential he is able to greet all dogs calmly, giving the signals that say he is friendly and offers no threat.

If you have a friend who has a dog of sound temperament, this is an ideal way to get your puppy used to social interactions. As he gets older and more established, you can widen his circle of canine acquaintances.

Training classes

A training class will give your Dogue the opportunity to work alongside other dogs in a controlled situation, and he will also learn to focus on you in a different, distracting environment. Both these lessons will be vital as your dog matures.

However, the training class needs to be of the highest calibre or you risk doing more harm than good. Before you go along with your puppy, attend a class as an observer to make sure you are happy with what goes on.

Find out the following:

- How much training experience do the instructors have?

- Are the classes divided into appropriate age categories?

- Do the instructors have experience training Dogue de Bordeaux or any of the other Mastiff breeds?

- Do they use positive, reward-based training methods?

If the training class is well run, it is certainly worth attending. Both you and your Dogue will learn useful training exercises; it will increase his social skills, and you will have the chance to talk to lots of like-minded dog enthusiasts.

A training class provides the opportunity to mix with other dogs in a controlled environment.

Training guidelines

The Dogue de Bordeaux is a thinking dog, and he likes to use his brain. However, he is not the easiest dog to motivate and he sees no point in carrying out monotonous, regimented exercises. You therefore need to get yourself into his mindset so you can produce rewarding results in training which will enhance your relationship with him and establish his role as a loyal and loving family companion.

You will be keen to get started but in your rush to get training underway, do not neglect the fundamentals which could make the difference between success and failure.

You need to find his 'on' and 'off' switches i.e. what motivates him and what makes him give

up – and then think of ways of making your training as much fun, and as positive as possible.

When you start training, try to observe the following guidelines:

Choose an area that is free from distractions so your puppy will focus on you. You can move on to a more challenging environment as your pup progresses.

Do not train your puppy just after he has eaten or when you have returned from exercise. He will either be too full, or too tired, to concentrate.

Do not train if you are in a bad mood, or if you are short of time. These sessions always end in disaster!

Providing a worthwhile reward is an essential tool in training. It is unusual for a Dogue to prefer a toy over food, so tasty treats will probably be your best option.

Choose high-value treats, such as cheese, cooked liver or sausage, in order to sustain your Dogue's interest.

If your Dogue is motivated by a toy, make sure it is only brought out for training sessions so that it gains added value.

Keep your verbal cues simple, and always use the same one for each exercise. For example, when you ask your puppy to go into the down position, the cue is "down", not "lie down, "get down", or anything else. Remember, your Dogue does not speak English; he associates the sound of the word with the action.

If your dog is finding an exercise difficult, break it down into small steps so it is easier to understand. A Dogue can be strong-willed so you need to think creatively and give frequent rewards.

Do not make your training sessions boring and repetitious; your Dogue will quickly lose concentration and will cease to co-operate.

Do not train for too long, particularly with a young puppy, who has a very short attention span, and always end training sessions on a positive note.

This does not necessarily mean getting an exercise right. If your pup is tired and making mistakes, ask him to do a simple exercise so you have the opportunity to praise and reward him.

You may well find that he benefits from having a break and will make better progress next time you try. Above all, make training fun so you and your Dogue enjoy spending quality time together.

First lessons

Like all puppies, a young Dogue de Bordeaux will soak up new experiences like a sponge, so training should start from the time your pup arrives in his new home.

Wearing a collar

You may, or may not, want your Dogue to wear a collar all the time. But when he goes out in public places he will need to be on a lead, and so he should be used to the feel of a collar around his neck. The best plan is to accustom your pup to wearing a soft collar for a few minutes at a time until he gets used to it.

Fit the collar so that you can get at least two fingers between the collar and his neck. Then have a game to distract his attention. This will work for a few moments; then he will stop, put his back leg up behind his neck and scratch away at the peculiar itchy thing which feels so odd.

Bend down, rotate the collar, pat him on the head

and distract him by playing with a toy or giving him a treat. Once he has worn the collar for a few minutes each day, he will soon ignore it and become used to it.

Remember, never leave the collar on the puppy unsupervised, especially when he is outside in the garden, or when he is in his crate, as it is could get snagged, causing serious injury.

Walking on the lead

This is a simple exercise but the Dogue is a very powerful dog so you will need to establish who is in control. You and your Dogue need to master the basics before problems with pulling arise.

Once your puppy is used to the collar, take him outside into your secure garden where there are no distractions.

Attach the lead and, to begin with, allow him to wander with the lead trailing, making sure it does not become caught on anything. Then pick up the lead and follow the pup where he wants to go; he needs to get used to the sensation of being attached to you.

The next stage is to get your Dogue to follow you, and for this you will need some treats. To give yourself the best chance of success, make sure the treats are high value so your Dogue is motivated to work with you.

Show him you have a treat in your hand, and then encourage him to follow you. Walk a few paces, and if he is walking with you, stop and reward him. If he puts on the brakes, simply change direction and lure him with the treat.

Next, introduce some changes of direction so your puppy is walking confidently alongside you. At this stage, introduce a verbal cue – "heel" – when your puppy is in the correct position. You can then graduate to walking your puppy outside the home, as long as he has completed his vaccination programme, starting in quiet areas and building up to busier environments.

Training strategy

Some young Dogues decide that pulling on the lead is a good option, and, in no time, the dog is taking you for a walk. This soon becomes an unpleasant experience, so it is important to adopt a strategy that makes your Dogue realise there is absolutely no percentage in pulling.

Restrict lead training to the garden in the initial stages so you are working in an environment that is free from distractions.

Walk a few paces, being very aware of any tension on the lead. If you feel the lead tighten and your Dogue is attempting to get ahead of you, stop, change direction, and set off again. Your Dogue needs to understand that pulling ahead has exactly the opposite effect to the one he wants. Rather than calling the tune, he has to co-operate with you.

Keep a good supply of tasty treats and remember: only reward – with food and with verbal praise – when he is walking on a loose lead by your side.

The mistake made by many owners at this stage is to use the treats to lure the dog into position rather than rewarding him for the correct behaviour.

Keep training sessions short, and when you are ready to venture into the outside world, do not be too ambitious to begin with.

Build up the level of distraction and the duration of lead walking only when your Dogue is consistently showing the behaviour you want.

The Dogue de Bordeaux is a powerful animal so good lead-walking manners are essential.

Come when called

The Dogue de Bordeaux enjoys being with his family and you are unlikely to lose track of where he is. However there are times when he will be distracted. There are so many enticing smells, places to explore, people and dogs to meet... He will never stray too far away, but he may get into the habit of coming in his own time unless you make the recall a rewarding exercise.

Your aim must be to make coming when called even more rewarding than anything else on your Dogue's personal agenda. This needs to be built up over a period of time, with lots of repetition so your Dogue sees you as a fun person who is always ready to reward him, rather than as an irate owner who is trying to spoil his fun.

Hopefully, the breeder will have laid the foundations simply by calling the puppies to "come" when it is dinnertime, or when they are moving from one place to another.

You can build on this when your puppy arrives in his new home, calling him to "come" when he is in a confined space, such as the kitchen.

This is a good place to build up a positive association with the verbal cue – particularly if you ask your puppy to "come" to get his dinner!

The next stage is to transfer the lesson to the garden. Arm yourself with some treats, and wait until your puppy is distracted. Then call him, using a higher-pitched, excited tone of voice.

At this stage, a puppy wants to be with you, so capitalise on this and keep practising the verbal cue, and rewarding your puppy with a treat and lots of praise when he comes to you.

Now you are ready to introduce some distractions. Try calling him when someone else is in the garden, or wait a few minutes until he is investigating a really interesting scent.

When he responds, make a really big fuss of him and give him extra treats so he knows it is worth his while to come to you.

If your puppy responds, immediately reward him with a treat. If he is slow to come, run away a few steps and then call again, making yourself sound really exciting.

Jump up and down, open your arms wide to welcome him; it doesn't matter how silly you look, he needs to see you as the most fun person in the world.

When you have a reliable recall in the garden, you can venture into the outside world. Do not be too ambitious to begin with; try a recall in a quiet place with the minimum of distractions so you can be more certain of success.

Do not make the mistake of only asking your dog to come at the end of his allotted exercise period. What is the incentive in coming back to you if all you do is clip on his lead, marking the end of his free time?

Instead, call your dog at random times, giving him a treat and a stroke, and then letting him go free again. In this way, coming to you – and focusing on you – is always rewarding.

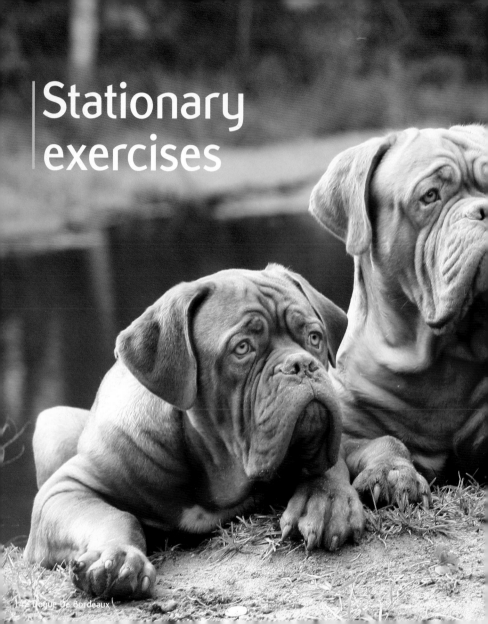

Stationary
exercises

The Sit and Down are easy to teach, and mastering these exercises will be rewarding for both you and your Dogue. You are dealing with a large, sometimes boisterous individual so it is useful if you have a means of bringing proceedings to a standstill before everyone gets carried away!

Sit

The best method is to lure your Dogue into position, and for this you can use a treat or his food bowl.

Hold the reward (a treat or food bowl) above his head. As he looks up, he will lower his hindquarters and go into a sit.

Practise this a few times and when your puppy understands what you are asking, introduce the verbal cue, "sit".

When your Dogue understands the exercise, he will respond to the verbal cue alone, and you will not need to reward him every time he sits. However, it is a good idea to give him a treat on a random basis when he co-operates to keep him guessing!

Down

This is an important lesson, and can be a lifesaver if an emergency arises and you need to bring your Dogue to an instant halt.

You can start with your dog in a sit or a stand for this exercise. Stand or kneel in front of him and show him you have a treat in your hand. Hold the treat just in front of his nose and slowly lower it towards the ground, between his front legs.

As your Dogue follows the treat he will go down on his front legs and, in a few moments, his hindquarters will follow.

Close your hand over the treat so he doesn't cheat and get the treat before he is in the correct position. As soon as he is in the down, give him the treat and lots of praise.

Keep practising, and when your Dogue understands what you want, introduce the verbal cue, "down".

Control exercises

These exercises are not the most exciting, but they are important in establishing a relationship of mutual respect with your Dogue de Bordeaux.

Wait

This exercise teaches your Dogue to wait in position until you give the next command.

The most useful application of wait is when you are getting your dog out of the car and you need him to stay in position until you clip on his lead.

Start with your puppy on the lead to give you a greater chance of success. Ask him to sit, and stand in front him. Step back one pace, holding your hand, palm flat, facing him.

Wait a second and then come back to stand in front

of him. You can then reward him and release him with a word, such as "OK".

Practise this a few times, waiting a little longer before you reward him, and then introduce the verbal cue, "wait". You can reinforce the lesson by using it in different situations, such as asking your Dogue to "wait" before you put his food bowl down.

Stay

This differs from the wait exercise as you want your Dogue to stay in position for a prolonged period. You need to differentiate this by using a different verbal cue.

Start with your Dogue in the down as he is most likely to be secure in this position. Stand by his side and then step forwards, with your hand held back, palm facing the dog.

Step back, release him, and then reward him. Practise until your Dogue understands the exercise and then introduce the verbal cue, "stay".

Gradually increase the distance you can leave your puppy, and increase the challenge by walking around him – and even stepping over him – so that he learns he must stay until you release him.

Leave/Off

These verbal cues are used for different scenarios but the principle remains the same. When you ask your dog to "leave" you are asking him to let go of what he is holding, whether it be a toy or a forbidden object, such as your best shoe!

When you give the verbal cue, "off", you are asking him to move, e.g. get off the sofa, bed or armchair. In both situations, you offer something equally good – which will generally be a high value treat – so that he is happy to oblige. This avoids confrontation, which is essential with a breed who can be assertive in his behaviour.

The "leave" command can be taught quite easily when you are first playing with your puppy. As you gently, take a toy from his mouth, swap it for another toy or a treat.

Do not try to pull the toy from his mouth if he refuses to give it up, as you will make the situation confrontational.

Let the toy go 'dead' in your hand, and then swap it for a new toy, or a really high-value treat so this becomes the better option.

When your Dogue understands the exercise, introduce a verbal cue, e.g. "leave".

Adopt the same policy if you want your dog to get off the sofa, for example show your Dogue you have a treat and lure him from the sofa. As soon as he co-operates, reward him with the treat. Keep practising and when your Dogue understands what you want him to do, introduce a verbal cue, e.g. "off".

Make sure you use high-value treats so your Dogue gets a reward that is worth having. Remember to make a big fuss of your Dogue when he does as you ask. Verbal praise – being in your good books – means a lot to a Dogue so never stint on giving him attention and telling him he is the best dog in the world!

Be creative in your training so you avoid confrontation.

Opportunities
for Dogue
De Bordeaux

The Dogue de Bordeaux is a clever dog and with consistent training, he will be a most reliable and trustworthy companion. He likes to see a reason for doing things, and is not a born enthusiast for extra curricular activities. However, if you get on his wavelength and motivate him, you may be surprised at your success!

Good Citizen Scheme

The Kennel Club Good Citizen Scheme was introduced to promote responsible dog ownership, and to teach dogs basic good manners.

In the US there is one test; in the UK there are four award levels: Puppy Foundation, Bronze, Silver and Gold.

Exercises within the scheme include:

- Walking on lead

- Road walking

- Control at door/gate.

- Food manners

- Recall

- Stay

- Send to bed

- Emergency stop.

Obedience

If your Dogue has mastered basic obedience, you may want to get involved in competitive obedience. The exercises include: heelwork at varying paces with dog and handler following a pattern decided by the judge, stays, recalls, retrieves, sendaways, scent discrimination and distance control. The exercises get progressively harder as you progress up the classes.

A Dogue will readily learn the exercises that are used in obedience competitions, but this is a discipline that calls for a very high degree of precision and accuracy which does not suit all dogs, or all handlers.

Rally O

If you do not want to get involved in the rigours of Competitive Obedience, you may find that a sport called Rally O is more to your liking.

This is loosely based on Obedience, and also has a few exercises borrowed from Agility when you get to the highest levels. Handler and dog must complete a course, in the designated order, which has a variety of different exercises which could number from 12 to 20. The course is timed and the team must complete within the time limit that is set, but there are no bonus marks for speed.

The great advantage of Rally O is that it is very relaxed, and anyone can compete; indeed, it has proved very popular for handlers with disabilities as they are able to work their dogs to a high standard and compete on equal terms with other competitors.

Showing

Exhibiting a dog in the show ring sounds easy but, in fact, it entails a lot of training and preparation.

Your Dogue will have to be calm and confident in the busy show atmosphere, so you need to work on his socialisation, and also take him to ringcraft classes so you both learn what is required in the ring.

Your Dogue will be subjected to a detailed 'hands on' examination by the judge; he must learn to stand still in a show pose and to move on a loose lead so the judge can assess his gait.

Showing at the top level is highly addictive, so watch out, once you start, you will never have a free date in your diary!

Training is all about spending quality time with your Dogue.

Health care

We are fortunate that the Dogue de Bordeaux is a healthy breed and with good routine care, a well-balanced diet, and sufficient exercise, most will experience few health problems.

However, it is your responsibility to put a programme of preventative health care in place, and this should start from the moment your puppy, or older dog, arrives in his new home.

Vaccinations

Dogs are subject to a number of contagious diseases. In the old days, these were killers, and resulted in heartbreak for many owners. Vaccinations have now been developed, and the occurrence of the major infectious diseases is now very rare. However, this will only remain the case if all pet owners follow a strict policy of vaccinating their dogs.

There are vaccinations available for the following diseases:

Adenovirus (Canine Adenovirus): This attacks the liver and affected dogs have a classic 'blue eye'.

Distemper: A viral disease which causes chest and gastro-intestinal damage. The brain may also be affected, leading to fits and paralysis.

Parvovirus: Causes severe gastro enteritis, and most commonly affects puppies.

Leptospirosis: This bacterial disease is carried by rats and affects many mammals, including humans. It causes liver and kidney damage.

Rabies: A virus that affects the nervous system and is invariably fatal. The first signs are abnormal behaviour when the infected dog may bite another animal or a person. Paralysis and death follow. Vaccination is compulsory in most countries. In the UK, dogs travelling overseas must be vaccinated.

Kennel cough: There are several strains of kennel cough, but they all result in a harsh, dry, cough. This disease is rarely fatal; in fact most dogs make a good recovery within a matter of weeks and show few signs of ill health while they are affected. However, kennel cough is highly infectious among dogs that live together so, for this reason, most boarding kennels will insist that your dog is protected by the vaccine, which is given as nose drops.

Lyme disease: This is a bacterial disease transmitted by ticks. The first signs are limping, but the heart, kidneys and nervous system can also be affected. The ticks that transmit the disease occur in specific regions, such as the north-east states of the USA, some of the southern states, California and the upper Mississippi region. Lyme disease is still rare in the UK so vaccinations are not routinely offered.

Vaccination programme

In the USA, the American Animal Hospital Association advises vaccination for core diseases, which they list as distemper, adenovirus, parvovirus and rabies. The requirement for vaccinating for non-core diseases – leptospriosis, lyme disease and kennel cough – should be assessed depending on a dog's individual risk and his likely exposure to the disease.

In the UK, vaccinations are routinely given for distemper, adenovirus, leptospirosis and parvovirus.

In most cases, a puppy will start his vaccinations at around eight weeks of age, with the second part given a fortnight later.

However, this does vary depending on the individual policy of veterinary practices, and the incidence of disease in your area.

You should also talk to your vet about whether to give annual booster vaccinations. This depends on an individual dog's levels of immunity, and how long a particular vaccine remains effective.

Parasites

No matter how well you look after your Dogue de Bordeaux, you will have to accept that parasites (internal and external) are ever present, and you need to take preventative action.

Internal parasites: As the name suggests, these parasites live inside your dog. Most will find a home in the digestive tract, but there is also a parasite that lives in the heart. If infestation is unchecked, a dog's health will be severely jeopardised, but routine preventative treatment is simple and effective.

External parasites: These parasites live on your dog's body – in his skin and fur, and sometimes in his ears.

Roundworm

This is found in the small intestine, and signs of infestation will be a poor coat, a pot belly, diarrhoea and lethargy. Pregnant mothers should be treated, but it is almost inevitable that parasites will be passed on to the puppies. For this reason, a breeder will start a worming programme, which you will need to continue. Ask your vet for advice on treatment, which will be ongoing throughout your dog's life.

Tapeworm

Infection occurs when fleas and lice are ingested; the adult worm takes up residence in the small intestine, releasing mobile segments (which contain eggs) that can be seen in a dog's faeces as small rice-like grains. The only other obvious sign of infestation is irritation of the anus. Again, routine preventative treatment is required throughout your Dogue's life.

Heartworm

This parasite is transmitted by mosquitoes, and so will only occur where these insects thrive. A warm environment is needed for the parasite to develop, so it is more likely to be present in areas with a warm, humid climate.

However, it is found in all parts of the USA, although its prevalence does vary. At present, heartworm is rarely seen in the UK. Heartworm live in the right side of the heart. Larvae can grow up to 14 inches (35.5cm) in length.

A dog with heartworm is at severe risk from heart failure, so preventative treatment, as advised by your vet, is essential. Dogs living in the USA should have regular blood tests to check for the presence of infection.

Lungworm

Lungworm, or *Angiostrongylus vasorum*, is a parasite that lives in the heart and major blood vessels supplying the lungs.

It can cause many problems, such as breathing difficulties, blood-clotting, sickness and diarrhoea, seizures, and can be fatal.

The parasite is carried by slugs and snails, and the dog becomes infected when ingesting these, often accidentally when rummaging through undergrowth. Lungworm is not common, but it is on the increase and a responsible owner should be aware of it.

Fortunately, it is easily preventable and even affected dogs usually make a full recovery if treated early enough. Your vet will be able to advise you on the risks in your area and what form of treatment may be required.

Fleas

A dog may carry dog fleas, cat fleas, and even human fleas. The flea stays on the dog only long enough to have a blood meal and to breed, but its presence will result in itching and scratching.

If your dog has an allergy to fleas, which is usually a reaction to the flea's saliva, he will scratch himself until he is raw.

Preventative treatment needs be administered on a routine basis; this can be in the form of a tablet, spot-on treatment, an insecticidal spray or shampoo.

Ask your vet for advice on what product to use. Bear in mind that the whole environment your dog lives in will need to be sprayed, and all other pets living in your home will also need to be treated.

How to detect fleas

You may suspect your dog has fleas, but how can you be sure? There are two methods to try.

Run a fine comb through your dog's coat, and see if you can detect the presence of fleas on the skin, or clinging to the comb. Alternatively, sit your dog on white paper and rub his back. This will dislodge faeces from the fleas, which will be visible as small brown specks. To double check, shake the specks on to some damp cotton wool (cotton). Flea faeces consists of the dried blood taken from the host, so if the specks turn a lighter shade of red, you know your dog has fleas.

Ticks

These are blood-sucking parasites which are most frequently found in rural areas where sheep or deer are present.

The main danger is their ability to pass lyme disease to both dogs and humans. Lyme disease is prevalent in some areas of the USA, although it is still rare in the UK. The treatment you give your dog for fleas generally works for ticks, but you should discuss the best product to use with your vet.

How to remove a tick

If you spot a tick on your dog, do not try to pluck it off as you risk leaving the hard mouth parts embedded in his skin. The best way to remove a tick is to use a fine pair of tweezers or you can buy a tick remover.

Grasp the tick head firmly and then pull the tick straight out from the skin. If you are using a tick remover, check the instructions, as some recommend a circular twist when pulling. When you have removed the tick, clean the area with mild soap and water.

Ear mites

These parasites live in the outer ear canal. The signs of infestation are a brown, waxy discharge, and your dog will continually shake his head and scratch his ear.

If you suspect your Dogue has ear mites, a visit to the vet will be needed so that medicated ear drops can be prescribed.

Fur mites

These small, white parasites are visible to the naked eye and are often referred to as 'walking dandruff'. They cause a scurfy coat and mild itchiness.

However, they are zoonetic – transferable to humans – so prompt treatment with an insecticide prescribed by your vet is essential.

Harvest mites

These are picked up from the undergrowth, and can be seen as a bright orange patch on the webbing between the toes, although this can be found elsewhere on the body, such as on the ears flaps.

Treatment is effective with the appropriate insecticide.

Skin mites

There are two types of parasite that burrow into a dog's skin. *Demodex canis* is transferred from a mother to her pups while they are feeding. Treatment is with a topical preparation, and sometimes antibiotics are needed.

The other skin mite, *Sarcoptes scabiei*, causes intense itching and hair loss. It is highly contagious, so all dogs in a household will need to be treated, which involves repeated bathing with a medicated shampoo.

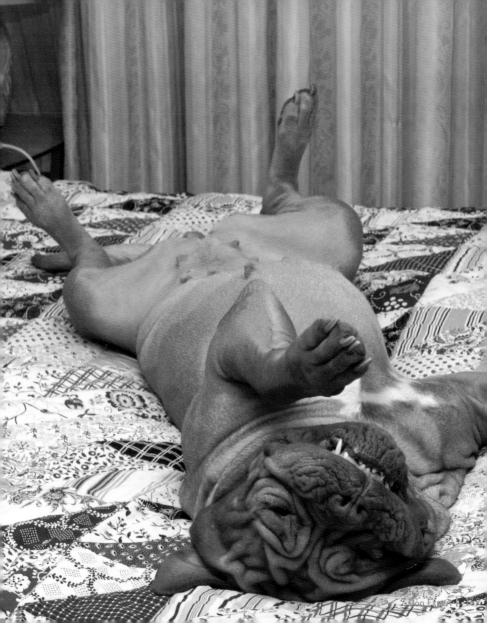

Common ailments

As with all living animals, dogs can be affected by a variety of ailments. Most can be treated effectively after consulting with your vet, who will prescribe appropriate medication and will advise you on how to care for your dog's needs.

Here are some of the more common problems that could affect your Dogue de Bordeaux, with advice on how to deal with them.

Anal glands

These are two small sacs on either side of the anus, which produce a dark-brown secretion that dogs use when they mark their territory. The anal glands should empty every time a dog defecates but if they become blocked or impacted, a dog will experience increasing discomfort.

He may nibble at his rear end, or scoot his bottom along the ground to relieve the irritation. Treatment involves a trip to the vet, who will empty the glands manually. It is important to do this without delay or infection may occur.

Dental problems

Good dental hygiene will do much to minimise gum infection and tooth decay, which is why teeth cleaning should be part of your regular care routine. If tartar accumulates to the extent that you cannot remove it by brushing, the vet will need to intervene. In a situation such as this, an anaesthetic will need to be administered so the tartar can be removed manually.

Diarrhoea

There are many reasons why a dog has diarrhoea, but most commonly it is the result of scavenging, a sudden change of diet, or an adverse reaction to a particular type of food.

If your dog is suffering from diarrhoea, the first step is to withdraw food for a day. It is important that he does not dehydrate, so make sure that fresh drinking water is available.

However, drinking too much can increase the diarrhoea, which may be accompanied by vomiting, so limit how much he drinks at any one time.

After allowing the stomach to rest, feed a bland diet, such as white fish or chicken with boiled rice, for a few days. In most cases, your dog's motions will return to normal and you can resume usual feeding, although this should be done gradually.

However, if this fails to work and the diarrhoea persists for more than a few days, you should consult you vet.

Your dog may have an infection which needs to be treated with antibiotics, or the diarrhoea may indicate some other problem which needs expert diagnosis.

Ear infections

The Dogue de Bordeaux has relatively small ears which lie close to the head. This means that air does not circulate as freely as with erect ears, which can create an environment for infection.

A healthy ear is clean with no sign of redness or inflammation, and no evidence of a waxy brown discharge or a foul odour.

If you see your dog scratching his ear, shaking his head, or holding one ear at an odd angle, you will need to consult your vet.

The most likely causes are ear mites, an infection, or there may be a foreign body, such as a grass seed, trapped in the ear.

Depending on the cause, treatment is with medicated ear drops, possibly containing antibiotics. If a foreign body is suspected, the vet will need to carry out further investigations.

Eye problems

The Dogue de Bordeaux has oval eyes, set well apart, which are neither sunken nor prominent. The third eyelid, should not be visible. Poor eyelid conformation, which does occur in the breed, predisposes the Dogue to cornea damage and infection.

If your Dogue's eyes look red and sore, he may be suffering from some form of infection or from conjunctivitis.

This may, or may not be accompanied with a watery or a crusty discharge. You will need to consult your vet for a correct diagnosis, but in the case of an infection, treatment with medicated eye drops is effective.

Foreign bodies

In the home, puppies – and some older dogs – cannot resist chewing anything that looks interesting. The toys you choose for your dog should be suitably robust to withstand damage, but children's toys can be irresistible. Some dogs will chew – and swallow – anything from socks, tights, and any other items from the laundry basket to golf balls and stones from the garden. Obviously, these items are indigestible and could cause an obstruction in your dog's intestine, which is potentially lethal.

The signs to look for are vomiting, and a tucked up posture. The dog will often be restless and will look as though he is in pain. In this situation, you must get your dog to the vet without delay, as surgery may be needed to remove the obstruction.

Heatstroke

The Dogue de Bordeaux has a short muzzle and flattened nose which is characteristic of all brachycephalic breeds. This type of conformation makes breathing more laboured, which, in turn, leads to an ineffective cooling system.

As a result the Dogue will over-heat easily and may suffer from heatstroke unless precautions are taken. If the weather is warm, make sure your Dogue has access to shady areas, and wait for a cooler part of the day before going for a walk. Be extra careful if you leave your Dogue in the car as the temperature can rise dramatically – even on a cloudy day. Heatstroke can happen very rapidly, and unless you are able to lower your dog's temperature, it can be fatal. If your dog appears to be suffering from heatstroke, lie him flat and work at lowering his temperature by spraying him with cool water and covering him with wet towels. As soon as he has made some recovery, take him to the vet, where cold intravenous fluids can be administered.

Lameness/limping

There are a wide variety of reasons why a dog can go lame, from a simple muscle strain, to a fracture, ligament damage, or more complex problems with the joints.

The Dogue de Bordeaux is a fast-growing breed, which then carries a lot of weight, so problems with lameness are not uncommon.

If you are aware that your Dogue is not moving soundly, do not delay in seeking expert advice. As your Dogue becomes more elderly he may suffer from arthritis, which is not uncommon in heavyweight breeds.

The signs are general stiffness, particularly when he gets up after resting. It will help if you ensure his bed is in a warm draught-free location, and if your Dogue gets wet after exercise, you must dry him thoroughly. If he seems to be in pain, consult your vet who will be able to help with pain relief medication.

Skin problems

If your dog is scratching or nibbling at his skin, first check he is free from fleas. There are other external parasites which cause itching and hair loss, but you will need a vet to help you find the culprit.

An allergic reaction is another major cause of skin problems. It can be quite an undertaking to find the cause of the allergy, and you will need to follow your vet's advice, which often requires eliminating specific ingredients from the diet, as well as looking at environmental factors.

Breed-
specific
disorders

Like all pedigree dogs, the Dogue de Bordeaux does have some breed-related disorders. If diagnosed with any of the diseases listed here, it is important to remember that they can affect offspring so breeding from such dogs should be discouraged.

There are now recognised screening tests to enable breeders to check for affected individuals and hence reduce the prevalence of these diseases within the breed. DNA testing is also becoming more widely available, and as research into the different genetic diseases progresses, more DNA tests are being developed.

Eye disorders

Canine multifocal retinopathy

In this condition abnormal patches or lesions appear on the retina; onset can be from as young as four months and usually both eyes are affected. Progression is variable and it may disappear altogether. Vision does not seem to be affected. A DNA test is available for potential breeding stock.

Ectropion

This is an inherited eye condition where the eyelid droops away from the eye and turns outwards. This ranges in severity from mild to the more serious, where surgical correction is required.

Gastric torsion

The breed can be predisposed to gastric torsion (bloat) as are several other deep-chested breeds of dog. Bloat is an extremely serious, life threatening condition. It usually occurs when there is an unusual accumulation of air, fluid and foam in the stomach. As the stomach swells it may rotate, twisting between the oesophagus and the upper intestine. The bloated stomach obstructs veins in the abdomen leading to low blood pressure, shock and damage to internal organs. Signs need to be spotted early and include gagging, foaming at the mouth and restlessness.

Immuno-deficiency syndrome

This results in a weakened immune response when required. In the Dogue de Bordeaux, a lack of B lymphpcyte cells in the immune system has been identified, resulting in recurrent bouts of respiratory and gastro-intestinal infections. Treatment is with antibiotics.

Heart conditions

Aortic stenosis

This involves a narrowing of the aortic valve in the heart which restricts blood flow. Symptoms may be mild but in severe cases, surgery may be required.

Diluted cardiomyopathy

This is a disease of the heart muscle that results in weakened contractions and poor pumping ability. As the disease progresses, the heart chambers become enlarged, and one or more of the valves may leak leading to heart failure.

Early signs are an intolerance to exercise, and a heart murmer may become evident.

Juvenile glomerulonephropathy

This is a kidney disease that has reported in several breeds including the Dogue de Bordeaux. Age of onset us usually under two years.

The disease is progressive and it is usually fatal. Signs include anorexia, dehydration, lethargy, weight loss and vomiting.

Joint disorders

Cruciate disease

Rupture or damage of the cruciate ligament may occur in the Dogue de Bordeaux. Quite often, the onset of lameness is sudden, in which case the dog will carry its foot, standing with it off the ground. Sometimes the lameness is intermittent, gradually worsening until the condition becomes apparent.

This can be operated on but the success of the operation depends very much on the critical aftercare of the patient.

Almost total confinement is imperative in the early post-operative period (a large crate is invaluable here) with only trips to the garden for toilet duty allowed, and even those on a lead. After this prolonged period of rest, limited exercise on a lead may be introduced, with an eventual return to carefully supervised natural exercise.

Hip dysplasia

This is a malformation of the hip joint where the head of the femur does not align with the cup of the hip socket. Resulting lameness ranges from mild to severe. Surgery can be effective. All potential breeding stock should be x-rayed and hip-scored.

Osteochondrosis (Ocd)

Osteochondrosis occurs in the giant and heavy breeds and is the result of abnormal cartilage development which causes a weakened area in the joint cartilage.

Often this weak area becomes partially detached and forms a flap in the joint space, or becomes fully detached and floats around in the joint area. Recent research reveals that a growing number of breeds are afflicted by osteochondrosis in the elbow, but this condition is also associated with the shoulder

However, with rest and confinement, the majority of animals make a full return to soundness without surgery. It is most important to maintain a balanced diet with a good quality dog food for the growing puppy, as there is every indication that this condition is aggravated by over-supplementation of calcium in the diet which the young puppy cannot expel in the way that a mature dog can.

Palmoplantar (footpad) hyperkeratosis

The outer layer (epidermis) of the foot pads harden and abnormal growths may develop. Cracks and secondary bacterial infections can lead to lameness.

Summing up

It may give the pet owner cause for concern to find out about health problems that may affect their dog. But it is important to bear in mind that acquiring some basic knowledge is an asset, as it will allow you to spot signs of trouble at an early stage.

Early diagnosis is very often the means to the most effective treatment. Fortunately, the Dogue de Bordeaux is a generally healthy and disease-free dog, with his only visits to the vet being annual check-ups. In most cases, owners can look forward to enjoying many happy years with this affectionate and highly entertaining companion.

Useful addresses

Breed & Kennel Clubs

Please contact your Kennel Club to obtain contact information about breed clubs in your area.

UK

The Kennel Club (UK)
1 Clarges Street London, W1J 8AB
Telephone: 0870 606 6750
Fax: 0207 518 1058
Web: www.thekennelclub.org.uk

USA

American Kennel Club (AKC)
5580 Centerview Drive, Raleigh, NC 27606.
Telephone: 919 233 9767
Fax: 919 233 3627
Email: info@akc.org
Web: www.akc.org

United Kennel Club (UKC)
100 E Kilgore Rd, Kalamazoo,
MI 49002-5584, USA.
Tel: 269 343 9020
Fax: 269 343 7037
Web:www.ukcdogs.com/

Australia

Australian National Kennel Council (ANKC)
The Australian National Kennel Council is the administrative body for pure breed canine affairs in Australia. It does not, however, deal directly with dog exhibitors, breeders or judges. For information pertaining to breeders, clubs or shows, please contact the relevant State or Territory Body.

International

Fédération Cynologique Internationalé (FCI)
Place Albert 1er, 13, B-6530 Thuin, Belgium.
Tel: +32 71 59.12.38
Fax: +32 71 59.22.29
Web: www.fci.be

Training and behavior

UK

Association of Pet Dog Trainers
Telephone: 01285 810811
Web: http://www.apdt.co.uk

Canine Behaviour
Association of Pet Behaviour Counsellors
Telephone: 01386 751151
Web: www.apbc.org.uk

USA

Association of Pet Dog Trainers
Tel: 1 800 738 3647
Web: www.apdt.com

American College of Veterinary Behaviorists
Web: www.dacvb.org

American Veterinary Society of Animal Behavior
Web: www.avsabonline.org

Australia

APDT Australia Inc
Web: www.apdt.com.au

For details of regional behaviorists, contact the relevant State or Territory Controlling Body.

Activities

UK
Agility Club
www.agilityclub.co.uk

British Flyball Association
Telephone: 01628 829623
Web: www.flyball.org.uk

USA
North American Dog Agility Council
Web: www.nadac.com

North American Flyball Association, Inc.
Tel/Fax: 800 318 6312
Web: www.flyball.org

Australia
Agility Dog Association of Australia
Tel: 0423 138 914
Web: www.adaa.com.au

NADAC Australia
Web: www.nadacaustralia.com

Australian Flyball Association
Tel: 0407 337 939
Web: www.flyball.org.au

International
World Canine Freestyle Organisation
Tel: (718) 332-8336
Web: www.worldcaninefreestyle.org

Health

UK
British Small Animal Veterinary Association
Tel: 01452 726700
Web: www.bsava.com

Royal College of Veterinary Surgeons
Tel: 0207 222 2001
Web: www.rcvs.org.uk

Alternative Veterinary Medicine Centre
Tel: 01367 710324
Web: www.alternativevet.org

USA
American Veterinary Medical Association
Tel: 800 248 2862
Web: www.avma.org

American College of Veterinary Surgeons
Tel: 301 916 0200
Toll Free: 877 217 2287
Web: www.acvs.org

Canine Eye Registration Foundation
The Veterinary Medical DataBases
1717 Philo Rd, PO Box 3007,
Urbana, IL 61803-3007
Tel: 217-693-4800
Fax: 217-693-4801
Web: www.vmdb.org/cerf

Orthopaedic Foundation of Animals
2300 E Nifong Boulevard
Columbia, Missouri, 65201-3806
Tel: 573 442-0418
Fax: 573 875-5073
Web: www.offa.org

American Holistic Veterinary Medical
Association
Tel: 410 569 0795
Web: www.ahvma.org

Australia
Australian Small Animal Veterinary
Association
Tel: 02 9431 5090
Web: www.asava.com.au

Australian Veterinary Association
Tel: 02 9431 5000
Web: www.ava.com.au

Australian College Veterinary Scientists
Tel: 07 3423 2016
Web: www.acvsc.org.au

Australian Holistic Vets
Web: www.ahv.com.au